ERNST KÄSEMANN

THE TESTAMENT OF JESUS

ERNST KÄSEMANN

THE TESTAMENT OF JESUS

A Study of the Gospel of John
in the Light of Chapter 17

FORTRESS PRESS

PHILADELPHIA

Translated by Gerhard Krodel
from the German
Jesu letzter Wille nach Johannes 17
published 1966 by J. C. B. Mohr (Paul Siebeck)
Tübingen

In Memory of Muriel S. Curtis

CONTENTS

ABBREVIATIONS

BZ	*Biblische Zeitschrift* (Paderborn)
ET	English translation
FRLANT	Forschungen zur Religion und Literatur des Alten und Neuen Testaments (Göttingen)
HzNT	Handbuch zum Neuen Testament, ed. H. Lietzmann (Tübingen)
JThC	*Journal for Theology and the Church* (New York)
KeK	Kritisch-exegetischer Kommentar über das Neue Testament (Göttingen)
NF	Neue Folge (=New Series)
NTD	Das Neue Testament Deutsch (Göttingen)
NTS	*New Testament Studies* (Cambridge)
SBT	Studies in Biblical Theology (London and Naperville)
ThLZ	*Theologische Literaturzeitung* (Leipzig)
ThR	*Theologische Rundschau* (Tübingen)
TU	Texte und Untersuchungen zur Geschichte der altchristlichen Literatur (Berlin)
ZNW	*Zeitschrift für die neutestamentliche Wissenschaft und die Kunde der älteren Kirche* (Berlin)
ZsystTh	*Zeitschrift für systematische Theologie* (Gütersloh)
ZThK	*Zeitschrift für Theologie und Kirche* (Tübingen)

PREFACE

THE LECTURES PUBLISHED here were given as the Shaffer Lectures at the Yale Divinity School on April 26–28, 1966. They endeavour to give an answer to the question which has interested me for almost forty years, namely, into which historical situation should the Gospel of John be placed? As early as my inaugural lecture at the University of Göttingen entitled 'Ketzer und Zeuger', I tried to find an answer. Since my solution proposed there was generally rejected, even by my friend Ernst Haenchen who repudiated it as a 'stroke of genius',[1] this made me hesitate for a long time and forced me to engage in self-criticism which resulted in relinquishing several too daringly constructed hypotheses. However, the intensive study of different Johannine interpretations as well as my own exegesis compelled me in the end to take up my former approach with modifications, limiting myself to the Gospel and pursuing my goal more thoroughly. One need not be a frog to jump twice into the same pond. Furthermore, my arguments are to a large extent not new, but only dug up again and properly aligned. Naturally, it is not my intention to discuss, much less to solve *all* the problems of the Fourth Gospel. While the question which I raise must keep the whole Johannine problem in mind, not every detail needs to be discussed. I am satisfied with probing into the centre of the complex of historical problems, either by taking the much-travelled route or by climbing along undiscovered paths. The wide landscape on both sides of the road can afterwards be surveyed anew.

My study is dedicated to the memory of a woman who, during the years 1947–8, preserved people totally unknown to her from hunger and collapse and who also made my theological work possible. Mrs Muriel S. Curtis represents that overwhelming hospitality which I experienced during more than eight months in my travels in the United States in 1965–6. To some of my new friends in the New World, these lectures may perhaps appear offensive and unsuitable as an expression of thanks. Anglo-Saxons are especially fond of the Gospel of John and radical criticism at this point may offend. But

---

[1] *ThR*, NF 26 (1960), pp. 281ff.

true dialogue depends on meeting, irritating and stimulating each other precisely where the stakes are the highest. A mere stroll over uncontroversial fields would seem to me inappropriate both to the riches of the impressions which I received in America and to my expectations from the impetuous new generation of young theologians.

I would like to thank my friend Professor Gerhard Krodel, of the Lutheran Theological Seminary in Philadelphia, for his well-considered translation.

Tübingen　　　　　　　　　　　　　　　　　　ERNST KÄSEMANN
Pentecost 1966

I

THE PROBLEM

I WOULD LIKE TO begin this study with the unusual confession that I shall be discussing a subject which, in the last analysis, I do not understand. Not without irony, one could point to the history of exegesis as offering the proof that only occasionally has exegesis achieved lasting results. If true understanding had actually been realized, then the great problems of New Testament interpretation would not need to become the object of diligent research in each new generation. But the enormous quantity of books and articles which are continuously appearing indicates that our interpretations only occasionally reach the desired goal. One could add the portentous generalization that everywhere in life true understanding is rather difficult and rare, while reciprocal misunderstanding usually characterizes the human situation.

The historian, however, should limit his horizons lest he substitute the general structures of life for concrete historical objects. I can therefore formulate my problem more precisely: Historical criticism has demolished the traditional opinion that the Fourth Gospel was written by John, the son of Zebedee. However, historical criticism has not offered us an acceptable substitute for that outdated view. All of us are more or less groping in darkness when we are asked to give information about the historical background of this Gospel, information which would determine our understanding of the whole book and not merely of individual details. Nowhere else in the New Testament do we find ourselves in a greater dilemma than in John, even though everywhere in the New Testament we encounter such riddles that introductions to the New Testament could, to a great extent, be placed into the literary genre of fairy tales, their dry tone or their pretence of factual reporting notwithstanding. The Evangelist whom we call John appears to be a man without definite contours.

We can hear his voice, a voice distinct from the rest of primitive Christianity, and yet we are unable to locate exactly his historical place. Much of what he says is quite understandable and frequently we are deeply moved by it. But his voice retains a strange other-worldly quality. Every age in the Church's history has felt that other-worldliness and for this reason has esteemed his Gospel especially. The historian, however, cannot be content with that. His work pre-supposes the categories of time and space. A world without shadows and historical contours cannot be investigated. He must be able to localize an historical object in order to recognize it. Men can stand only when they have ground under their feet and this ground is also the presupposition of understanding. But here lies our problem: In a way, since the second century, the interpreters of the Fourth Gospel have been endeavouring to discover the forgotten historical situation in which this Gospel arose. The numerous conflicting and, to a sur-prising extent, diametrically opposed interpretations prove better than anything else that the quest for the historical situation of the Fourth Gospel has so far been unsuccessful. This is not to deny that new possibilities of understanding are continually opened up, possibilities which in part raise real issues and in part mark new progress which cannot be surrendered. But, on the other hand, im-partial analysis will also establish that sheer fantasy and ignorance are just as busily and continuously reburying what others have dug up. The purpose and the chaos of scholarship are here reflected equally[1] and only a few participants show serious concern because of it. Historically, the Gospel as a whole remains an enigma, in spite of the elucidation of individual details.[2]

It is the intention of my lectures at least to contribute to the recognition of this fact as a challenge addressed to us. To be sure, experience might teach us that there is little hope of mastering at long

[1] In this connection we should not forget the work of F. Overbeck, *Das Johannes-evangelium* (1911). He comments sarcastically on p. 79, 'Modern scholarship in the case of the Gospel of John is like a bear dependent on licking its own paws to get something.' Similarly J. Wellhausen, *Das Evangelium Johannis* (1908), p. 3, 'We strain at the gnat and swallow the camel.'

[2] R. E. Brown, *The Gospel according to John*, Vol. I (1966), pp. cxxvif., would find little support for his affirmation that in view of the New Testament's diversity, it is not difficult to locate John within the mainstream of Christian thought. C. H. Dodd is more correct when he says in *The Interpretation of the Fourth Gospel* (1953), p. 6, 'There is no book, either in the New Testament or outside it, which is really like the Fourth Gospel', or E. Hirsch, *Das vierte Evangelium* (1936), p. 145, 'It is really that book of the New Testament which has sealed itself most tightly against superficiality.'

last that which lies unconquered before us.[3] But the historian can as little resist the fascination of tackling unsolved problems as a mountain-climber can resist the challenge of the peak rising before him. Experience will teach him that he will have to seek more audacious paths, if those that were followed in the past did not lead to the goal. Yet it is also true that the bolder the paths, the deeper could be the fall. But new endeavours could also open up new vistas. At least they can enable us to recognize the magnitude of the problem more clearly. Even if nothing else were gained, such an endeavour would not be in vain. For the raising of the right questions (because the difficulties are recognized more clearly) is the necessary beginning of scholarship and frequently its most important result.

John 17 serves as the basis and guidepost of my lectures. Regardless of how the question of the original position of this chapter is answered, it is unmistakable that this chapter is a summary of the Johannine discourses and in this respect is a counterpart to the prologue. It should be rewarding to unroll the problem of our Gospel almost, as it were, from the end, beginning with chapter 17. Of course, this cannot be done now in a detailed exegesis. I shall rather select certain key words from the context in which the distinctive Johannine themes are focussed and I shall analyse these themes; namely, the glory of Christ, the community under the Word, and Christian unity. They are treated successively, even though they are so closely interwoven in chapter 17, as well as in the whole Gospel, that they cannot be isolated from each other. Repetitions as well as omissions therefore cannot be avoided in this type of argumentation. The Johannine eschatology will be treated under the aspects of christology, ecclesiology and soteriology. However, a theological interpretation of the Fourth Gospel is not our ultimate aim. Rather, I shall unfold the complex of theological problems only so far as it can serve as a key for the historical question of the historical situation out of which this Gospel grew. The theological problems must, after all, point to a specific sector of primitive Christian history and, conversely, we must be able to deduce it from them.[4]

[3] E. C. Hoskyns, *The Fourth Gospel* (1947), pp. 20, 49f., endeavours to show that, on principle, the encounter with eternity conceals the historical situation and he accuses historical criticism of a lack of understanding in this matter. However, each encounter with eternity is bound up with a specific situation.

[4] So also R. Schnackenburg, *Das Johannesevangelium* I (1965), pp. 101, 134f.

II

THE GLORY OF CHRIST

IN THE COMPOSITION of chapter 17, the Evangelist undoubtedly used a literary device which is common in world literature and employed by Judaism as well as by New Testament writers. It is the device of the farewell speech of a dying man.[1] Its Jewish antecedents are represented by the Testaments of the Twelve Patriarchs. Within the New Testament this device is found in the farewell speech of Paul to the elders of Ephesus in Miletus (Acts 20), in the pseudonymous tract known as II Timothy describing the ideal bishop, and in the eschatological tract known as II Peter. It was also introduced into the story of Jesus' passion, where, in Mark 13, it served to provide a place for apocalyptic material. In Mark 13, Jesus, as he went to his death, anticipated his disciples' future in prophecy, warning and reassurance. If the Fourth Gospel took up this Synoptic tradition, then John transformed it to an unusual extent. For apocalyptic instruction, which dominates the testament of Jesus in Mark 13, has disappeared from John. In its place we find four long chapters, roughly one-fifth of the whole Gospel, which are connected by the motif of the farewell discourse and which thus received an importance unsurpassed even by John's passion and resurrection narratives.

What prompted John to emphasize this form of presentation? It is not sufficient to answer that the farewell discourses were composed as a clever transition to the concluding section of his work. For this form of presentation is essentially paradoxical. The whole Gospel pictures Jesus not merely as a miracle-worker who heals the sick, raises the dead and remains unassailable by his enemies, but also as the one in whom eternal Life and Resurrection appear personified. A

[1] Compare E. Stauffer, *Die Theologie des Neuen Testaments* (1948), pp. 327ff. (ET *New Testament Theology* [1955], pp. 344ff.); W. Bauer, *Das Johannesevangelium* (1933), pp. 207f.; O. Michel, 'Das Gebet des scheidenden Erlösers', *ZsystTh* 18 (1941), pp. 521–34.

testament in the mouth of the Prince of Life is, however, most unusual and we can hardly suppose that the Evangelist failed to reflect
on this paradox. Therefore we must investigate the basis and the
purpose of his manner of presentation. Why did he choose to clothe
his thoughts in the form of a testament? The first thing we recognize is
that here the Evangelist was marking an epoch not merely in the life
of Jesus, but also in the history of the community. This can be seen
in the fact that John 17, in distinction to the previous chapters, was
composed in the form of a prayer. Again, this is not merely the
clever use of a literary device. For the prayer of Jesus does not play
the same important role in John as in the Synoptics, and John 11.41f.
gives us the reason for it. Jesus has no need to ask the Father because
his request is always heeded at once. Thus actually he can only give
thanks. His prayer, therefore, differs from ours in that, like his discourses, it, too, witnesses to his unity with the Father. He lives in
royal freedom and in the certainty of his immediacy to the Father
and therefore he has no more care. To be sure, John 17 contains
individual petitions, but it does not become a prayer of supplication.
Rather, his majestic 'I desire' dominates the whole chapter. This is
not a supplication, but a proclamation directed to the Father in such
manner that his disciples can hear it also. The speaker is not a needy
petitioner but the divine revealer and therefore the prayer moves
over into being an address, admonition, consolation and prophecy.
Its content shows that this chapter, just like the rest of the farewell
discourse, is part of the instruction of the disciples. The presentation
of the instruction in the form of the prayer, however, indicates that
the disciples' fate does not rest in their own hands. The decision
about them has been made in heaven, and the Johannine Christ
appeals to the throne of God on their behalf that this decision may
remain in force. In this respect, he exercises that intercession which
in Rom. 8.34 and in the Letter to the Hebrews belongs to the
heavenly High Priest who has been exalted to the right hand of the
Father. In John, the disciples become witnesses to the dialogue
between the Son and the Father, in which their future course is
being determined, and thus they themselves are drawn into a fundamentally heavenly activity. The one who speaks here is, in the last
analysis, not the one who is about to die. The dying of Jesus comes
into view only as the presupposition of the farewell situation, of his
departure from the earth. Therefore this chapter is not a testament
in the sense of a last will and bequest, but rather in the sense of a

final declaration of the will of the one whose proper place is with the Father in heaven and whose word is meant to be heard on earth. In a certain sense, the proclamation of the eternal gospel, spoken of in Rev. 14.6, is also taking place here. To be sure, in John 17 and Rev. 14, the situation, the content and the recipients differ from each other, but in both instances we encounter the motif of a heavenly proclamation, concise in form and ultimate in significance.[2]

Here a new problem arises. John 17, like the farewell discourses in general and in contrast, for instance, to the Sermon on the Mount, is a secret instruction to the disciples. Its scope encompasses the total earthly history. But only the disciples can hear it and understand it. Insight which the world cannot and may not have is granted to them, even though the message as such is not enigmatic. It is no accident that in v. 3 the key word 'gnosis' already appears. Apparently this 'gnosis' does not refer to the anthropological and cosmological mysteries as they are communicated through apocalyptic proclamation. Nevertheless, the truth with which we deal here, the knowledge and acceptance of which places man under obligation, is revealed only to the enlightened and the elect and is therefore communicated in the form of a secret discourse. The community addressed is actually joined more closely to heaven than to earth. Even though it still exists in earthly form, it belongs in its very essence to the realm of the Father and the Son.

These introductory remarks will have to suffice to indicate the peculiar atmosphere in which the problems of the Fourth Gospel arise. We shall now focus our attention on the text itself. The beginning of John 17 is dominated by the key word 'glorification' of Jesus. With this key word, the message of the whole Gospel is taken up once more in our chapter. The prologue in 1.14 has already summarized the content of the Gospel with 'We beheld his glory'.[3] Consistently with this, the book closes with the confession of Thomas (20.28), 'My Lord and my God', and with a reference to the many other signs and miracles of Jesus which could be reported. It has always been recognized that no other Gospel narrates as impressively as John the confrontation of the world and of the believers with the glory of Jesus,

[2] The prayer is therefore neither an integral part of Christ's enthronement, as stated by T. Arvedson, *Das Mysterium Christi* (1937), pp. 132f. and C. H. Dodd, *op. cit.*, pp. 419ff., nor should it be limited (see Hoskyns, *op. cit.*, pp. 494ff.) to a prayer of consecration.

[3] See my article, 'Aufbau und Anliegen des johanneischen Prologs', in *Exegetische Versuche und Besinnungen* II (1964), pp. 155–80.

even in the passion story. In view of this it is astonishing that even though Jesus' glory is recognized as being already manifest, nevertheless at the same time, in a certain respect, it is also regarded as still being in the future, for his glory will be perfected only with his death.[4] What is astonishing is not so much the tension between both affirmations as such. We find this in many other parts of the New Testament, inasmuch as we meet there the phenomenon of a twofold eschatology, of realized and futuristic eschatology. Its intention is to proclaim the end of the world as already breaking into the earthly present reality now with Christ. The twofold eschatology is connected with christology elsewhere in the New Testament in that the earthly Jesus is distinguished from the returning Judge of the world, or the crucified one is distinguished from the resurrected and exalted Lord. In short, John stands here within a firm tradition, but, as is his custom otherwise, he develops this tradition further in an astonishing and even paradoxical manner. While Paul and the Synoptics also know the majesty of the earthly Jesus, in John the glory of Jesus determines his whole presentation so thoroughly from the very outset that the incorporation and position of the passion narrative of necessity becomes problematical. Apart from a few remarks that point ahead to it, the passion comes into view in John only at the very end. One is tempted to regard it as being a mere postscript which had to be included because John could not ignore this tradition nor yet could he fit it organically into his work. His solution was to press the features of Christ's victory upon the passion story. At any rate he does not describe the journey of Jesus as a process which leads from lowliness to glory. Despite the stress on the agreement in structure between John and the Synoptics, especially in Anglo-Saxon scholarship, John is hardly based on a pattern according to which the Galilean teacher enters Jerusalem with Messianic honours before he is shown hanging shamefully on the cross, then, in an abrupt change of fortune, to appear in the glory of the resurrection. Of course, John knew of this tradition and did not despise its pattern when it appeared useful or necessary to him. But he employs it with the greatest freedom and ruthlessly breaks it up when his viewpoint demands it. Therefore the cleansing of the temple is found at the beginning of Jesus' activity and many journeys to Jerusalem take place for various feasts. The miracle of the raising

---

[4] This problem dominates the investigation of W. Thüsing, *Die Erhöhung und Verherrlichung Jesu im Johannesevangelium* (1960).

of Lazarus opens and is the cause of the passion. Theological themes dominate the structure of this Gospel. It is obvious that the category of the Galilean teacher does not apply to the one who, like a mystagogue, with long-drawn-out monologues, symbolic speeches and cryptic intimations confronts the world, provokes its misunderstandings and precipitates its judgment. Neither historical reminiscences nor a concentration on Jesus' own development dominate the writing of the Fourth Gospel. Certainly one can and must raise the question how far this Gospel is parallel to the Synoptics and how much it reflects their emphasis in its details.[5] But if this is done in the interest of showing the closest possible approximation between John and the Synoptics, rather than of drawing the contrast between them, then the peculiar Johannine accents and stresses are shifted and the interpretation falls under the domination of apologetics. Here, as in other places, one can see that the victory march of historical criticism became possible within the field of New Testament scholarship only because fundamental questions had not been thoroughly discussed. The method was confined to tackling surface problems with an attempt at harmonization, rather than a quest for different nuances and divergent viewpoints. Historical criticism has won a total victory today because it turned out that it could successfully be domesticated *ad usum Delphini*. Its task is then no longer to lay bare offences and trouble-spots, to indicate the problems involved in traditional viewpoints, but rather to undergird the conservative approach, bringing it into an advantageous position at a stage prior to actual theological investigation and thus drawing the teeth of radical higher criticism at the earliest moment. Nowadays, the battles are often fought in the theatre, using blank cartridges. The 'happy ending' is not merely wishful thinking, but the condition tacitly agreed upon for the historical-critical enterprise, and even satires of this technique of transformation would offend against good manners. The Gospel of John is the favourite playground for such practice.

What customary scholarship endeavours methodologically, namely to show that John approximates to or complements the Synoptic tradition, is then expressed in practice, quite remarkably, through the almost universal attempt to find a christology of humiliation even in the Fourth Gospel. It is typical that a discussion based on the kind of liberal interpretation which characterizes the Johannine Christ as

---

[5] Cf. C. H. Dodd, *Historical Tradition in the Fourth Gospel* (1963), as representative of this.

God going about on the earth[6] is generally omitted, or confined to comments on exegetical details. Yet here we meet one of the most important issues, if not the decisive problem of Johannine interpretation. Unless this problem is dealt with thematically, the suspicion arises that one has not even recognized it. Problems cannot be replaced, like clothing, simply by creating a new fashion. The problem of the divine glory of the Johannine Christ going about on earth is not yet solved, but rather most strikingly posed when we hear the declaration of the prologue: 'The Word became flesh.' For what reasons is this statement almost always made the centre, the proper theme of the Gospel? Of course, it introduces and establishes the possibility of writing the earthly story of Jesus. However, we must also ask: In what sense is he flesh, who walks on the water and through closed doors, who cannot be captured by his enemies, who at the well of Samaria is tired and desires a drink, yet has no need of drink and has food different from that which his disciples seek? He cannot be deceived by men, because he knows their innermost thoughts even before they speak. He debates with them from the vantage point of the infinite difference between heaven and earth. He has need neither of the witness of Moses nor of the Baptist. He dissociates himself from the Jews, as if they were not his own people, and he meets his mother as the one who is her Lord. He permits Lazarus to lie in the grave for four days in order that the miracle of his resurrection may be more impressive. And in the end the Johannine Christ goes victoriously to his death of his own accord. Almost superfluously the Evangelist notes that this Jesus at all times lies on the bosom of the Father and that to him who is one with the Father the angels descend and from him they again ascend. He who has eyes to see and ears to hear can see and hear his glory. Not merely from the prologue and from the mouth of Thomas, but from the whole Gospel he perceives the confession, 'My Lord and my God'. How does all this agree with the understanding of a realistic incarnation? Does the statement 'The Word became flesh' really mean more than that he descended into the world of man and there came into contact with earthly existence, so that an encounter with him became possible?[7] Is not this statement totally overshadowed by the confession 'We beheld his glory',[8]

---

[6] F. C. Baur, *Kritische Untersuchungen über die kanonischen Evangelien* (1847), pp. 87, 313; G. P. Wetter, *Der Sohn Gottes* (1916), p. 149; E. Hirsch, *op. cit.*, p. 138, represent this view.

[7] So F. C. Baur, p. 97.

[8] So again F. C. Baur, pp. 94ff.

so that it receives its meaning from it? I am not interested in completely denying features of the lowliness of the earthly Jesus in the Fourth Gospel. But do they characterize John's christology in such a manner that through them the 'true man' of later incarnational theology becomes believable?[9] Or do not those features of his lowliness rather represent the absolute minimum of the costume designed for the one who dwelt for a little while among men,[10] appearing to be one of them,[11] yet without himself being subjected to earthly conditions? His death, to be sure, takes place on the cross, as tradition demands. But this cross is no longer the pillory, the tree of shame, on which hangs the one who had become the companion of thieves. His death is rather the manifestation of divine self-giving love and his victorious return from the alien realm below to the Father who had sent him.

This line of argumentation is not contradicted by pointing out that the Fourth Gospel clearly speaks of the obedience of the one whom the Father has sent.[12] It cannot be denied that we meet here the tradition of a christology of humiliation as known to us through Phil. 2.7f. It is, however, questionable whether John would permit us to base on that tradition an interpretation of the whole Gospel in terms of a christology of humiliation. Not even Paul should be understood in this way, as if Christ's obedience were, for Paul, merely the sign of his lowliness. For according to Rom. 5.12ff., Christ as the obedient one is at the same time the new Adam and the heavenly *anthropos*. Correspondingly, for John obedience is the mark of the Son of Man who not only participates in the mission of God, but also fulfils it. He finds his food in the fulfilment of the divine will, a food which exempts him from earthly food, and unites him with the Father. Therefore in John, the obedience of the earthly Jesus is not, as in Phil. 2.9, rewarded with his exaltation,[13] but rather is finished and brought to a close by his return to the Father. Obedience is the form

[9] As examples of this view see E. C. Hoskyns, *op. cit.*, pp. 17f., and C. H. Dodd, *Interpretation*, p. 249. But more or less all modern interpretations of John follow this line, dominated by the idea of the incarnation.

[10] Cf. 'He tabernacled among us' (1.14), which is taken up by the paradoxical 'a little while' of the farewell discourses in 14.19; 16.16ff.; as already in 7.33; 12.35; 13.33.

[11] The misunderstandings in 6.42; 7.27; 7.35f.; 8.48, 53; 9.29; arise from the problem of the humanity of Jesus.

[12] As is done by E. Haenchen, 'Der Vater, der mich gesandt hat', *NTS* 9 (1962/3) pp. 208–16, and earlier by Dodd, *Interpretation*, p. 254.

[13] Thüsing's interpretation is completely oriented on the pattern of Phil. 2.6ff. In this orientation may lie the decisive error of his investigation (see Thüsing, *op. cit.*, p. 223).

and concretion of Jesus' glory during the period of his incarnation. During this time the divinity he claims is misunderstood, provokes objection and requires a final revelation. The formula 'the Father who sent me' is, lastly, neither the only nor the most typical christological formula in the Gospel. The Baptist, too, according to 1.6, is 'sent by God'. To be sent by God means, to begin with, nothing else than 'to be authorized'. Yet, according to the rabbinic maxim, the delegate is the representative of the sender and as such the recipient must accept him as equal to the sender. In the Gospel, the formula 'the Father who sent me' therefore alternates continuously with the concept of the oneness with the Father, and the former receives its peculiar christological meaning through the latter. Jesus is the heavenly messenger who acts out of his oneness with the Father. In unique dignity as the Father's 'exegete' (1.18), he surpasses everyone else who may otherwise have been sent. A truly subordinationist christology can by no means be deduced from this, regardless of how relevant the distinction between the Father and the Son might be for John. This distinction is, however, important for his concept of revelation, which holds that there is no access to the Father except through Jesus and, correspondingly, that Jesus has no other function and authority apart from being the revealer of God. If the formulae of his commission through the Father and his unity with the Father are isolated from each other, the result will be subordinationism or ditheism. Both formulae are correlative and complementary, because only together do they describe the truth that Jesus is nothing but the revealer and, on the other hand, that Jesus is the only revealer of God and therefore belongs totally on the side of God even while he is on earth.

The road travelled by the Johannine Christ should consequently not be presented as a development from lowliness to glory. But may we then speak instead of the paradox of a glory hidden in lowliness? Such an interpretation is commonplace today.[14] It is again surprising how rarely the basic problems of the interpretation of the Fourth Gospel are carefully thought through. In general, the interpretation is so greatly interested in balancing the extremes of possible explanations that it eagerly grasps for formulae which permit the establishment of a dialectical balance.[15] It is precisely through this

[14] Typical representatives are Hoskyns, *op. cit.*, pp. 81f.; C. K. Barrett, *The Gospel according to St John* (1955), p. 77.

[15] This approach is reflected in T. W. Manson, *On Paul and John* (1963), pp. 131ff., 152ff., where history and dogmatics, experience of love and metaphysics, divinity and humanity subjected to it are brought into balance.

method that the greatest danger arises. One-sided interpretations usually dig their own graves, or else they start a discussion leading to their correction. But dialectical formulae, such as the paradox of lowliness and majesty, are so vague and grant so much leeway to our understanding, that all sorts of different divergent notions can be attached to them. Clarity of thought is then replaced by the fascination exercised by the slogans. It is obvious that a real paradox between the lowliness and the glory of the earthly Jesus can only be affirmed if we seriously speak about Jesus' afflicted humanity exposed to the world, to suffering and to death.[16] The disguise, the hiding, of a divine being in lowliness may appear paradoxical, but it is not really paradoxical at all. Such concealment, in the last analysis, is to make communication possible between what is unequal and therefore separate, between heaven and earth, God and man. As the possibility of communication such hiding is something very proper and very purposeful and quite rationally understandable. It indicates condescension, but not antinomy. It is, of course, right to argue that the notion of Jesus' humiliation is found also in the Fourth Gospel, because his mission necessitated his descent from heaven to earth and this descent, his humiliation, is brought to an end through his return. But lowliness and glory, humiliation and exaltation, do not remain separated like two stages on a journey, so that when one is here one cannot be there. They are rather united with each other in that the earthly Christ who enters the world of suffering and death does not lose his unity with the Father. He does not really change himself, but only his place. Human fate is thrust upon him so that in a divine manner he may endure it and overcome it. Individual development cannot take place for the one who is himself the way, that is to say who is both the beginning and the goal for his followers, the resting place for those whose hearts are troubled without him. Because he himself is the Life and the Resurrection, the world of suffering and death has no power over him even in his dying. To him the Father has given power over all things. The world is for him only a point of transit and humiliation simply means being in exile. His humanity may time and again arouse misunderstanding and offence. However, it is not his humanity as such which does so, but rather his humanity as the medium of the call to acknowledge the Creator by believing

[16] The notion of the paradox is thought through in this sense only by R. Bultmann; cf. *Die Theologie des Neuen Testaments* (5th ed., 1965), pp. 399f. (ET *Theology of the New Testament* II [1955], pp. 47f.).

in the Son. The combination of humiliation and glory is not paradoxical as such, because the humiliation makes the epiphany and presence of glory possible and represents its concretion. Only the exclusive, absolute claim through which Jesus binds salvation to his message and person is offensive and paradoxical.

The Synoptic writers, Paul and even Hebrews endeavoured to find a balance between the cross and the exaltation, and they have done so in various ways. John is, to our knowledge, the first Christian to use the earthly life of Jesus merely as a backdrop for the Son of God proceeding through the world of man and as the scene of the inbreaking of the heavenly glory.[17] Jesus is the Son of Man because in him the Son of God comes to man.[18] It is characteristic of John's radical reinterpretation that he uses this title which designated the apocalyptic World Judge to refer to the earthly existence of Jesus. The Son of Man is neither a man among others, nor the representation of the people of God or of the ideal humanity,[19] but God, descending into the human realm and there manifesting his glory. Eighteen centuries have been fascinated by this picture of the Johannine Christ, and in their faith have concurred with the prologue and the confession of Thomas. The Church of all ages acknowledges the statement 'We beheld his glory', and consequently accepts the Gospel which illustrates this sentence.

We have taken a long detour in order to grasp adequately the problem of John's characteristic of a twofold eschatology and the christology resulting from it. The usual beginning is to point out the preponderance of the so-called present or realized eschatology which is a special characteristic of the Gospel. In this connection, the question of the frequency and importance of the remnants of a futurist eschatology remains controversial. It is acknowledged that John knows no imminent expectation nor a cosmic drama of the end in the sense of apocalypticism. His place in the third Christian generation shows itself in the reduction of futurist eschatology to the realm of anthropology. This holds true, even if the present form of the Johannine text is regarded as original, that is, if those texts dealing with the future resurrection are not excluded as later interpolations.

[17] We must therefore (contrary to Barrett, *op. cit.*, p. 58) speak of a 'higher' christology, if we cannot follow Barrett, p. 77, in emphasizing the humanity and the subjection of Jesus to the Father.

[18] Cf. R. Schnackenburg, 'Der Menschensohn im Johannesevangelium', *NTS* 11 (1964–1965), pp. 123–37.

[19] Contrary to Dodd, *Interpretation*, p. 248.

Since ch. 21 does testify to a redactional revision of this Gospel, the possible presence of interpolations within the rest of John cannot simply be excluded. A point in favour of regarding the futurist texts as interpolations is the fact that these are only a few verses which are cast into stereotyped form and are detached from the theological complex as well as from the context. But even if the text is accepted in its traditional form, we still have no more than a few meagre relics of pre-Johannine beliefs which do not constitute a real counter-balance to specifically Johannine ideas but merely restrain their extreme development. In that case, the Evangelist would have failed to outgrow completely the relics of the past and would have retained the individual hope of a future resurrection when he forsook the apocalyptic expectation of the imminent end and of the arrival of the new world.[20] We shall see later that such an interpretation is not totally impossible.

The problems touched on here force us to reflect more thoroughly upon the specifically Johannine proclamation at this point. We see its peculiarity in 5.24, which states most emphatically that the believer 'has already passed from death to life'. The following verse underlines this: 'The hour is already here when the dead shall hear the voice of the Son of God and those who hear it will live.' John 3.36; 6.47; 8.51; 11.25f. state with the same certainty that eternal life is now already present in the believer. This eternal life cannot even be touched by earthly death. John 3.18ff. draws a line from here to the extremely radical statement that the final judgment, which had traditionally been expected to happen on the last day, has happened already with the coming of Jesus who, in John 11.25, personifies the Resurrection and the Life. We have been accustomed to understanding sentences such as these in an edifying, more or less 'spiritual' manner,[21] and to tone down their cutting edge by harmonizing and balancing them with the Church's futurist eschatology. In doing this, however, we fail to recognize the apparently polemical character of the Johannine proclamation and its eschatology as it is expressed, for instance, in ch. 11. Above all, we also generally fail to see or at least to express the fact that statements like this grow out of a firm tradi-

---

[20] H. Strathmann, *Das Evangelium nach Johannes* (1954), p. 18: 'Eschatological thinking has achieved a permanent footing in the Church's thought.'

[21] E. Gaugler, 'Die Bedeutung der Kirche in den johanneischen Schriften', *Internationale kirchliche Zeitschrift* 14 (1924), pp. 97–117; 181–219; 15 (1925), pp. 27–42, interprets this in a liberal vein (p. 112): 'For the loving community the concept of a final judgment has disappeared.' But in that case, what about the concept of the final resurrection of the dead?

tion which the New Testament frequently preserved. We meet this tradition in the baptismal proclamation of Col. 2.12f. and Eph. 2.5f., where it is even connected with a statement about the heavenly enthronement. The pre-Pauline existence of such traditions in Hellenistic enthusiasm is also confirmed by Rom. 6.4ff., where Paul takes up that tradition and modifies it by changing our resurrection and life with Christ from the perfect tense into the future tense. With respect to the present, our resurrection with Christ has, for Paul, only a metaphorical meaning and validity, namely as a figurative expression of the new obedience of the Christian. The *Sitz im Leben* of this view becomes quite clear when enthusiastic members of the Corinthian congregation reject, not Christ's resurrection, but the believer's future resurrection. Undoubtedly they held this view because they thought that through baptism they already participated in the resurrection world and eternal life, and therefore could contemptuously encounter earthly death. Our chain of historical evidence is complete when II Tim. 2.18 counters this heretical proclamation that the resurrection of the dead has already taken place. It is quite disturbing that the Evangelist, at the very centre of his proclamation, is dominated by a heritage of enthusiasm against which Paul had already struggled violently in his day and which in the post-apostolic age was branded as heretical. John, however, was too independent and too critical to accept without modifications a heritage which in the deutero-Pauline writings had already been adjusted to the Church's eschatology. John detached it from the context of the understanding of baptism as an initiation into mysteries and placed it in the service of his christology. The *praesentia Christi* is the centre of his proclamation. After Easter this means the presence of the Risen One. All the Gospels presuppose Easter, and therefore they develop a post-Easter christology of Jesus as the Son of God. It may also be right to say that all the Gospels understand Jesus' miracles in the light of Easter, whether in the sense that bodily healing sets men on the horizon of the dawning new world, or else in the sense that the power of the miracle-worker is interpreted as the energy of the divine spirit and the power of the resurrection. John's account is not totally new, but it does have radical consequences. Not only is it presented from the perspective of the resurrection of the dead which had been anticipated in Jesus' resurrection, but it also affirms what the enthusiasts of Corinth and the heretics of II Tim. 2.18 had proclaimed, namely that the reality of the general resurrection of the dead is already present now. The reason for this affirmation lies in the fact that Jesus is known only in his resurrection existence. Unlike Luke, John has not yet learned to understand Jesus' resurrection as an individual event limited to Jesus only. At this point he remains faithful to the apocalyptic view which he otherwise left behind and holds that Jesus' resurrection is the beginning of the general resurrection of the dead. But he forsakes the apocalyptic view in that he no longer separates the beginning from the end, but rather, like the Corinthian enthusiasts, has the beginning and end focussed in, and coinciding with, the today of the presence of Christ. The world of the resurrection has broken into this earth with Christ and is present only within the realm of Christ's influence. There, however, the resurrection is present in such manner that the believers, too, are grasped by it and reborn. Earthly death is insignificant wherever Christ appears. The man who belongs to Christ still has this death before him and around him, just as he still must sleep. Yet this is only the appearance and the shadow of the power of death which has already been overcome. The reality of death lies behind the believer, even if, like Lazarus, he should still die. In the presence of Christ, the reality and the threat of death no longer exist. We must continually keep in mind that John does not understand this metaphorically, spiritually or as edifying oratory. John's point of departure here is not his anthropology, so that one could argue that in this case the believer's hope is proleptically anticipated. Rather, his point of departure is his christology. Its reality is seen in Christ's world-wide victory over all his enemies, as expressed in various christological hymns of the New Testament. Wherever Christ is encountered, man has come into the realm of his victory and participates in it so long as he remains in this realm as a believer. The shift in eschatology becomes apparent. Primitive Christian eschatology was prepared through the message and activity of Jesus and constituted through Easter, and in this sense the primitive eschatology was always christologically oriented. For John, however, eschatology is no longer the force that determines christology; the opposite is the case. Christology determines eschatology and eschatology becomes an aspect of christology. In Christ, the end of the world has not merely come near, but is present and remains present continually.

If this is so, then the distinction, gained from cosmology and anthropology, between realized and futurist eschatology in the Gospel of John can be maintained only with difficulty, and, in the last analysis, is no longer appropriate. This distinction no longer characterizes the centre of Johannine theology but, at most, its periphery. Therefore, time and again John's interpreters have had to note the pre-eminence of so-called realized eschatology and regard the futurist statements as last testimonies, or as relics of an older tradition which are trailing along, but are no longer an organic part of John's theology, or even to delete them as glosses. Bultmann's famous formulation[22] that Easter, Pentecost and the Parousia coincide in John is absolutely correct from the perspective of John's christology. At most, one could find fault with Bultmann's formulation because it does not recognize the complexity of the situation. His remark does not indicate that in John the earthly life of Jesus also belongs to this category. But Bultmann could never include Jesus' earthly life in it, because he interpreted the Johannine incarnation radically as an entry into a totally human life. His interpretation is oriented on the pattern of humiliation-exaltation and he sees both concepts paradoxically related to each other. But can one really avoid that pattern? Even if the career of Jesus may not be understood as a process of development and growth and even if the use of the catchword 'paradox' becomes questionable in view of the emphasis on the divinity of Jesus, one must still agree that John speaks of Jesus' glory both as present reality and future reality. Furthermore, in John the passion appears as the peculiar and proper hour of his glorification. The interpretation which dwells on the lowliness and humility of the earthly Jesus refers to this fact as its strongest support.[23] There is no real clarification of the eschatology and the christology of the Fourth Gospel so long as no precise understanding has been attained at this particular point. Consequently we return once more to our initial question and formulate the problem anew: In what relationship does Jesus' earthly life stand to his passion, and, furthermore, what is the nature and character of his passion if the resurrection and the life already appear in the earthly Jesus?

The second question receives its answer in that the comprehensive and, for John, characteristic description of Jesus' death is given with

[22] Bultmann, *Theologie*, p. 410 (ET II, p. 58).

[23] So especially in Thüsing, *op. cit.*, pp. 46, 48ff., 201ff., who consequently postulates two 'time-spans' of Jesus' glory. He sees the first under the sign of his death, pp. 100, 192, and the second under the sign of his 'new status', p. 207. Of necessity he thus regards the glory of the pre-existent one as problematical. Similarly Dodd, *Interpretation*, p. 208, who interprets the earthly glory under the aspect of love. Similarly W. Bauer, *Johannesevangelium*, p. 203, and Barrett, *op. cit.*, p. 418.

the verb *hypagein*, to go away. This verb includes exaltation and glorification in so far as it refers to the separation from the world and the return to the Father, which is at the same time the return to the glory of the pre-existent Logos. The aspect of his obedience is not eliminated here. On the contrary, obedience is and must be constitutive because through it his passion is connected with his earthly life. From this perspective, Jesus' death, in the Fourth Gospel as in Phil. 2.6ff., is the completion of his incarnation. But in distinction from Phil. 2.9, the exaltation in John does not appear as a divine reward for the earthly obedience rendered, and one should avoid contrasting earthly obedience with exaltation.[24] John himself uses neither the noun 'obedience' nor the verb 'to obey'. Instead he has the formula 'to do the will', which corresponds to the other formula, 'to hear the word'. We may paraphrase both with 'obedience', but it should then be clear to us that this may not be understood moralistically,[25] and above all that it has nothing to do with what we usually mean by humility.[26] Instead, both formulae express a commitment to the heavenly realm, to remaining in that truth which opposes subjection to the power and deceit of the earthly realm. If we want to call this obedience, then lowliness is expressed through it only in so far as this commitment to the heavenly realm and to the divine truth must exist on earth, seeking life with God in conflict with the earthly rebellion against God. Obedience is then the manifestation of the divine Lordship, of the divine glory, in the realm below which is alienated from God. For Christ, obedience is the attestation of his unity with the Father during his sojourn on earth. For this reason Jesus' passion must be described as a triumphal procession in John instead of a *via dolorosa*. Lowliness in John is the nature of the situation, of the earthly realm which Jesus entered. In entering it, he himself is not being humbled. He retains the glory and majesty of the Son until the cross. There once more he judges his judges as he has always done before. When he is given up by the Father, he demonstrates more clearly than ever that the earth has no power over him.[27] In summary: The glory of Jesus is not the result

---

[24] Contrary to Hoskyns, *op. cit.*, pp. 449f., 464. According to him the earthly life of Jesus is separation from the Father.

[25] Contrary to Barrett, *op. cit.*, pp. 60, 72; Thüsing, *op. cit.*, p. 239.

[26] Contrary to Barrett, *op. cit.*, p. 262.

[27] Therefore I find it impossible to agree with R. Bultmann, *Das Evangelium des Johannes* (1941), p. 377, that the glorified one is always the incarnate one, if this statement is interpreted to mean: 'The Exalted One is the lowly one and the humiliation and lowliness is not extinguished with the return to the heavenly *doxa*.'

of his obedience, so that, as in other New Testament writings, his glory could be defined from the perspective of his obedience. On the contrary, obedience is the result of Jesus' glory and the attestation of his glory in the situation of the earthly conflict.

If this is so, then the Johannine phrase 'the hour of Jesus' may not be interpreted as being nothing but a reference to his passion.[28] John 2.4; 4.21, 23; 5.25, 28 refer beyond doubt primarily to his hour of glorification, while 7.30; 8.20; 12.23, 27; 13.1; 17.1 refer primarily to his passion. But these two sets of references are not unconnected. In John 12.23; 13.1; 17.1 the hour of his passion is in a unique way the hour of the glorification of Jesus and from this viewpoint we can include all references to the hour of his passion as being allusions also to the hour of his glorification. But again this use of 'the hour' in John does not indicate that in the passion the humility of Jesus or his communion of love with the Father are most thoroughly realized,[29] nor does it indicate that, paradoxically, the exaltation begins in the deepest humiliation. John 13.1 clearly interprets the meaning of the passion. The hour of the passion and death is in a unique sense the hour of his glorification because in it Jesus leaves the world and returns to the Father.[30] Here we can see the result of our investigation thus far. John distinguishes the earthly glory of Jesus from that glorification which takes place in the passion. But this distinction is not a contrast and could not be one, because for John the earthly Jesus already personified the Resurrection and the Life. But neither is the earthly glory an anticipation of the glory bestowed on him in the exaltation;[31] at any rate, the catchword 'anticipation' does not express what is decisive in John at this point. The misunderstandings of the interpreters have their origin in an uncritical transfer of the pattern of a 'now already—not yet' eschatology to Johannine christology. One cannot, of course, object to this transfer as a working hypothesis, and historically it may even indicate the origins of John's christology, but everything depends on a correct insight into the modifications made by the Evangelist. The pattern of the 'now already—not yet' eschatology is christologically shattered by placing the glory of his pre-existence beside the glory of his earthly life and of

---

[28] Thüsing, *op. cit.*, pp. 76ff.; O. Cullmann, *Urchristentum und Gottesdienst* (1950)' p. 67 (ET *Early Christian Worship*, SBT 10 [1953], p. 66).
[29] Contrary to Dodd, *Interpretation*, pp. 208, 262; Thüsing, *op. cit.*, p. 182.
[30] In this respect, the death of Jesus does have the character of a centre of gravity, contrary to Bultmann, *Theologie*, p. 405 (ET II, p. 52).
[31] Contrary to J. Dupont, *Essais sur la Christologie de St Jean* (1951), p. 273.

his passion. More precisely, John understands the incarnation as a projection[32] of the glory of Jesus' pre-existence and the passion as a return to that glory 'which was his before the world began'. The glory of the earthly Jesus manifests itself in time and space and in a world of rebellion against God. In this respect, features of lowliness are connected with his glory. His glory is perfected through his death, since limitations cease and the realm of lowliness is left behind. This Johannine view really has nothing in common with the old futurist eschatology. The one who walks on earth as a stranger, as the messenger sent by the Father, the one who passes through death without turmoil and with jubilation, because he has been called back to the realm of freedom, has fulfilled his mission, as his last word from the cross indicates. Neither the incarnation nor the passion in John have those emphases and contents which were taken from ecclesiastical tradition. They do not mark a change in Christ according to his nature, but only a change in terms of 'coming' and 'going', of descending and ascending. Incarnation and passion indicate the change of space and thus of the scope of the manifestation of Christ. Since all his words and deeds manifest his being, always and everywhere, the one who reveals himself in them is the one who is always and everywhere one with the Father, the pre-existent Logos in his heavenly glory. If we wish to characterize this truth on the basis of the pattern of a twofold eschatology, then we may no longer regard the tension of the suffering and of the exalted Jesus as constituting the centre of that eschatology. In that case, the centre must rather be sought in the relationship of the eternal Logos to the revelation in the earthly Jesus. In John's eschatology, in so far as it is christology, the direction has been reversed, so that his eschatology no longer emphasizes the end and the future, but the beginning and the abiding. Because it is measured by the eternal, the temporal therefore has the character of the transitory. The basic problem is no longer the sense in which the crucified one is the Son of God, but rather the reason why God came into the flesh and gave himself to death. The answer to this question is given with the two words, mission and return.

We cannot register this change in perspective without raising the historical question as to the factors which made the change possible. We have already stated that John was dependent on an enthusiastic piety which affirmed a sacramentally realized resurrection of the dead in the present. To be sure, John unfolded his own proclamation

32 I am using an expression of Dodd, *Interpretation*, p. 262.

of the resurrection not from the sacrament but from his christology. Beginnings for this perspective can be found in the primitive Christian tradition. Already prior to John, hymns that had developed within the same enthusiastic piety described Jesus as a pre-existent heavenly being whose earthly existence was but a stage of a journey to take him back to heaven. Some of these hymns supplemented the mythological picture by transferring to Jesus the attribute of the mediator of creation as found in the Jewish Sophia myth. In so doing, they gave content and weight to his pre-existence. In this way a protology, a doctrine of the first things, was placed beside the eschatology,[33] and the latter was reflected in the former. Now the presupposition had been created for the centre of gravity to shift. When the place of the apocalyptic eschatology was taken by some sort of balance between protology and eschatology, then eventually the protology could move into the centre of the Christian message. Jesus then had to become the divine mediator of creation who came near to man in the incarnation and withdrew again from him in his passion. It is exactly this view which is consistently developed in our Gospel and which is made into the dominant motif.

From this point of view, the tradition of the miracle stories is transformed. For John, too, miracles are indispensable. They are not merely concessions to human weakness.[34] If that were the case, it would have been unnecessary to heighten them to the very extreme. Nor would Jesus' passion, with deliberate intention and contrary to all traditions, have been triggered off by the miracle of the raising of Lazarus. It would also ignore the fact that the Johannine miracles in general are clearly and emphatically described in terms of demonstrations of the glory of Jesus. Human need is, to be sure, the occasion for the miracle, but the meeting of human needs is at most a subsidiary aim. God does not manifest himself on earth without the splendour of the miracles which characterize him as the Creator. It is indeed correct to point out that John attacks a craving for miracles. This is not done, however, on the basis of a criticism of miracles in general, but in the interest of his one and only theme, namely, his christology. His dominant interest which is everywhere apparent is that Christ himself may not be overshadowed by anything, not even by his gifts, miracles and works. Jesus alone is the true divine gift to

[33] Cf. H. Hegermann, *Die Vorstellung vom Schöpferungsmittler im hellenistischen Judentum und Urchristentum* (1961).
[34] Contrary to Bultmann, *Theologie*, p. 409 (ET II, p. 56).

which all other gifts can and should only point. The isolated miracle is, from this perspective, just as illegitimate as the isolated sacrament, the Old Testament absolutized over against Christ, or the fathers and the witnesses in so far as an independent significance is ascribed to them. The presence of the miracles narrated by John cannot be explained by John's faithfulness toward the tradition. John took up that tradition freely. It was not accidental that he omitted demon exorcisms as not being illustrative enough of Jesus' glory and that he selected the most miraculous stories of the New Testament. He would hardly have done so had he wanted to use them as mere illustrations to the speeches of Jesus and thus been disinterested in the miracle itself. We must not forget that Thomas is referred to the faith which does not see, only after he has seen and touched. The intention here is to bind his faith to the word which conveys Jesus as the personified Resurrection, and not to isolated facts of salvation. At this point, interpreters generally modernize more than is permissible for the historian. No Christian at the end of the first century could have come to the idea that God could enter the human scene without miracles, or that the rebirth should be the sole miracle which is appropriate to him. The Johannine criticism of miracles begins and ends where Jesus himself is sought or forgotten for the sake of his gifts. On the other hand his glory cannot be without miracles and the greater and the more impressive they are the better. For his community confesses: 'From his fulness have all received grace upon grace.' There is no reductionism about the miracles in the Fourth Gospel!

Like the miracles, John's discourses are composed on his christological theme, which is also their centre and to a large extent their only content. Certainly the Evangelist collected the christological titles in order to present through them the different aspects of the universal significance of Jesus. But just as certainly they are all brought in line with the Johannine declaration of the unity of the Son with the Father. The possibility of misunderstanding this declaration is clearly brought out when the Jews regard it as blasphemy and when even the disciples are unable truly to understand, right up to the end. But the misunderstanding does not only cling to the declaration as such. It is misunderstood and ambiguous, like the miracles, because here, as in the miracles, the stranger from the world above reveals himself, while the world below continuously seeks to capture him in the net of its own categories and experiences. Regardless of how many features of the Hellenistic miracle-worker were transferred to the

Johannine Christ, he is still not a Son of God as that age understood it. For in that case he would have sought his own glory, and his unity with the Father would then have dissolved. Consequently, it is not his intention as a heavenly being to gain acceptance into the company of the great founders of religions who have come in their own name. For only as God's revealer does he remain one with the Father. Through him God is glorified, because only through him does it become clear who God is, namely, our Creator. His unity with the Father has a soteriological function. Only the one who is sent can reveal the one who has sent him. Only in the Son does the Father show himself as acting and speaking. Christ is the only 'exegete' of him whom no one else has ever seen. We shall have to ask later what that means concretely. Now we must recognize not only the exclusiveness of these declarations but also John's willingness to employ mythological language to express that exclusiveness. Once again, all attempts at modernization at this point grasp John's message only inadequately.[35] While the insight that the unity with the Father has soteriological functions is correct, it is insufficient to state merely that. The soteriological function remains the spearhead of the kerygma, but it now receives a tremendous new depth. With the christological mystery is connected what later times called the mystery within the Trinity. If this is true, however, then the mythology used in the Fourth Gospel, in distinction from the other New Testament writings, no longer merely has the purpose of proclaiming the world-wide and saving-historical dimension of the christological event. The Johannine mythology is at the same time an expression of the beginning of dogmatic reflection in the strictest possible sense and thus opens the door for patristic christology.[36] The problem of the nature of Christ is discussed thematically in John, to be sure still within the frame of his soteriology, but now with an emphasis and a force which can no longer be explained on the basis of a purely soteriological interest. The internal divine relationship of the revealer as the Son is just as strongly emphasized as his relation to the world.[37]

[35] This even includes Dupont, *Essais*, pp. 231, 267ff., 287f., who plays off mission against nature; Bultmann, *Theologie*, p. 414 (ET II, p. 62), who takes offence at the mythological notion of pre-existence; also all interpretations of the unity between Father and Son in terms of love.

[36] The embarrassment of the modern exegete is illustrated in T. W. Manson, *op. cit.*, who on p. 131 speaks of 'a dogmatic reconstruction cast into the form of history', whereas on p. 134 he states that, nevertheless, John stands closer to Paul than to Nicaea. Such triviality means nothing, even if Nicaea is relevant at all.

[37] Contrary to T. W. Manson, *op. cit.*, p. 135; Dupont, *op. cit.*, pp. 287f.

In this way, the exclusiveness of Jesus as the revealer receives its foundation and its safeguard.

The dogmatic emphasis of John is reflected even in the style of his discourses. In distinction from the Synoptics, the Johannine discourses are not collections of originally separate sayings, but rather lengthy monologues, which, under various aspects, revolve time and again around the same centre of the divine mission and nature of Jesus. Dogmatic reflection is their cause, meditation their form, definition their peculiar and outstanding feature. Movement enters into them almost exclusively through polemic, and the polemic is expressed through the literary device of absurd misunderstandings. Only in Paul do we find the same passionate theological discussion. But while the actual life of the Pauline communities evoked the problems with which Paul dealt, the discourses of John show the reverse. In John, a theological complex of dogma is forced upon the everyday life of the community with unmistakable harshness. A dogmatic controversy is taking place.[38] This controversy is directed against Judaism, as one would expect if the controversy is to be carried on by the earthly Jesus. At the end of the first century, there was ample reason for it, not only in Syria. On the other hand, we may not forget that in the Fourth Gospel the Jews are the representatives of the world as it is comprised by its religious traditions. The controversy with the Jews as the representatives of the world, therefore, has an exemplary significance for a larger, more extensive religious realm. At least we shall have to be more careful than in the past in evaluating the possibility that a struggle within the Church is reflected and hidden in these debates with the Jews. Such evaluation is all the more meaningful and mandatory if the origin of the Fourth Gospel in such circles of Hellenistic enthusiasm as are opposed both by I Cor. 15 and II Tim. 2.18 should prove to be correct. This does not mean that our Gospel had to be written against representatives of a different christology. It could well be that John was endeavouring to combat a development in the Church which in his opinion did not take christology sufficiently into account. If so, the controversy dealt with the slogan *solus Christus*, Christ alone. We cannot yet answer that question, but we shall take it up later in a different context.

If the unity of the Son with the Father is the central theme of the Johannine proclamation, then that unity is of necessity also the proper

---

[38] Wellhausen, *op. cit.*, p. 53, and Wetter, *op. cit.*, pp. 96, 169f., were already correct here.

object of faith. Nowhere else in the New Testament is faith described with such force, repetition, and dogmatic rigidity. Faith means one thing only; to know who Jesus is.[39] This knowing is not merely theoretical, for it verifies itself only in remaining with Jesus. Nor does it take place in one single act of perception from which everything else would automatically follow. It means discipleship, following on that way which is Jesus himself, following through a hostile world. In this pilgrimage it is necessary time and again for Jesus to come to us, promising, calling to remembrance, teaching, warning and comforting, and it is necessary for us time and again to recognize and acknowledge him anew. Such a description of the *fides qua creditur* should not, however, prompt us to try to define the confession of faith exclusively on the basis of the situation of decision. Neither our experience nor our decision determine who Jesus is. This is always established already for us as the *fides quae creditur*, as dogma, and therefore it can be formulated in a manner which transcends the situation of personal decision. John does not present us with a model of a Christianity without dogma. John's peculiarity is that he knows only one single dogma, the christological dogma of the unity of Jesus with the Father. Therefore one should not play off the kerygma against the dogma.[40] John neither proclaims the veneration of a new god, nor does he demand mere assent to the Church's dogma, even though God's revelation may have hitherto been hidden and Christian faith may be formulated in doctrinal statements. The reason why the individual believer is not in danger of losing himself to a philosophical world-view or a religious tradition or a Church dogmatics lies in the fact that his salvation is based on Jesus alone. Precisely for this reason, it may not be left to the individual to determine who Jesus is, otherwise world-views, religious traditions, and the ever-changing Church dogmatics would be at their most dangerous. Faith does not limit itself to theology and theology cannot guarantee faith, much less be a substitute for it. Without theology, however, faith cannot be kept alive and proclamation cannot rightly be made. All theology, even if it does not want to admit it, deals with dogma, because theology must remain related to the Jesus who was prior to our faith, and theology has to formulate who this Jesus was and is.

John did that in his own manner. In so doing he exposed himself

---

[39] Barrett, *op. cit.*, p. 58; Brown, *op. cit.*, p. LXXVIII; and earlier F. C. Baur, *op. cit.*, p. 183.

[40] Contrary to Bultmann, *Evangelium*, pp. 213, 298, 412.

to dangers which are an element of life and also of theology. One can hardly fail to recognize the danger of his christology of glory, namely, the danger of docetism.[41] It is present in a still naïve, unreflected form and it has not yet been recognized by the Evangelist or his community. The following Christian generations were thoroughly enchanted with John's christology of glory. Consequently the question 'Who is Jesus?' remained alive among them. But those generations also experienced the difficulties of this christology of glory and had to unfold and deepen its problems and, in so doing, had to decide for or against docetism. We, too, have to give an answer to the question of the centre of the Christian message. From John we must leran that this is the question of the right christology, and we have to recognize that he was able to give an answer only in the form of a naïve docetism. Thus we ourselves are forced to engage in dogmatics. An undogmatic faith is, at the very least, a decision against the Fourth Gospel.

[41] F. C. Baur, *op. cit.*, pp. 233, 286, 291, 373; Wellhausen, *op. cit.*, p. 113; Overbeck, *op. cit.*, pp. 30, 344, 364f.; Hirsch, *op. cit.*, pp. 8of. The assertion, quite generally accepted today, that the Fourth Gospel is anti-docetic is completely unproven.

III

THE COMMUNITY UNDER THE WORD

O NE OF THE many surprising features of the Fourth Gospel and perhaps the most surprising of all is that it does not seem to develop an explicit ecclesiology. By formulating the problem in this way, I am already indicating that I cannot conceive that Christian proclamation, including proclamation in the form of a Gospel in which christology is central, could be without ecclesiology. However, John does not unfold the kind of ecclesiology which the historian would expect to find in a representative of the Christian Church at the end of the first century. We cannot fail to see that even Luke made the epoch of the Church the centre of history and that Ephesians gave an impressive theological basis to this concept. Can John's proclamation neglect a theology of the Church when it so strongly emphasizes the glory of Jesus as a result of its orientation on the exalted Lord? Can it neglect a theology of the Church when it represses the apocalyptic hope as a result of being part of the trend towards early catholicism? It would be wrong to object that we should not expect a doctrine of the Church in a narrative of the earthly history of Jesus, since such a doctrine could only be introduced with difficulty. For after all, John changes the Galilean teacher into the God who goes about on earth;[1] would he not also be capable of picturing the circle of disciples from the perspective of the later church organization, as was done in part even by the Synoptic writers? Apparently the Fourth Gospel does not share in this development. Even the basic elements of congregational life, worship, the sacraments and ministry, play such insignificant roles that time and again John's interest in them has been doubted. Just

[1] Thus J. Grill, *Untersuchungen über die Entstehung des vierten Evangeliums* I (1902), p. 36; W. Heitmüller, *Das Johannesevangelium* (Die Schriften des Neuen Testaments IV, ³1918), pp. 11, 27.

as the concept 'Church' is absent, so are the titles of honour such as the 'family' or the 'people of God', the 'heavenly building' or the 'Body of Christ'. Correspondingly, the disciples seem to come into focus only as individuals,[2] and all the titles of honour which we miss with reference to the church organization are applied to them as individuals. They are the friends of Jesus, the beloved of God, the elect, those who are sanctified through the Word. They belong to the realm of truth, of light and life, in short, they belong to heaven. The same idea is present in Ephesians, which also set the Christian community in the heavenly sphere. All these observations have often been made already. Therefore it is all the more surprising that here, too, interpreters of the Gospel are usually satisfied to make the observations without dealing with the historical and theological problems inherent in them. Alternatively, they are more interested in harmonizing and striking a balance with the customary primitive Christian views than in analysing the 'concrete, the individual, the peculiar' features as F. C. Baur[3] so urgently demanded. Historical criticism has become a gadget for anyone to use. It no longer testifies to the passion and the intellectual horizon of the historian for whom tradition as such has become questionable, but now shows that texts can be manipulated by the specialists. Therefore, before dealing with our theme, we must be aware of and resist efforts of apologetics which endeavour to level off and gloss over the peculiar and the unique.

In the Fourth Gospel, too, Peter is regarded as the representative of the historical circle of disciples. John 20.6ff. still contains a slight indication that Peter's position is connected with the tradition that he was the first witness of the resurrection. Odd as it may seem, this connection is not brought out in a manner corresponding to the importance of the tradition. On the contrary, the resurrection stories in John tell of Mary Magdalene, of all the disciples and of Thomas, but are silent about Peter. Can this really be unintentional, especially when we remember the events of 20.4ff.? It is not Peter, but the other disciple (who is probably meant to be the Beloved Disciple), who reached the tomb first, and yet it is Peter who first enters it. Is the purpose of this last comment to strike a balance with the historical

---

[2] D. Faulhaber, *Das Johannesevangelium und die Kirche* (1935), pp. 51, 58f., 65; E. Schweizer, 'Der Kirchenbegriff im Evangelium und den Briefen des Johannes', *Studia Evangelica* (1959), p. 371 [also in *Neotestamentica* (1963), p. 254] (ET in *New Testament Essays: Studies in Memory of T. W. Manson*, ed. A. J. B. Higgins [1959], pp. 230ff.); Bultmann, *Theologie*, p. 444 (ET II, pp. 91f.).

[3] Baur, *op. cit.*, p. 75.

tradition? If so, the introduction of the Beloved Disciple means that here, too, the Petrine tradition is placed in the shadow of the Beloved Disciple. Whatever may be the significance of the Beloved Disciple elsewhere, it is obvious that he obscures the significance for the Church of the Prince of the Apostles.[4] Peter no longer towers above the other disciples, as is shown in exemplary fashion in 20.21. There all disciples receive in like manner the commission, the Holy Spirit and the authority to forgive or retain sins. The Johannine community has and acknowledges an office effected by the Spirit and endowed with specific authority. The commission given by Jesus leads not only into the world but also into the community, to its service, and even to its discipline. Our Gospel presupposes an organized communal life, and with the absolution it also takes for granted the institution of an office through the risen Lord. However, this office is not reserved for Peter, nor for the circle of apostles—the word apostle in its technical sense does not even occur in John—and therefore does not have to be transmitted through delegation by the apostles, as in the Pastorals. Interpretations of John 20.21 have often read the closed circle of 'the twelve' into the text.[5] John, however, speaks of the disciples. It is typical of his Gospel that it introduces new figures like Philip, Nathaniel, Nicodemus, Lazarus, Thomas, and—what is especially significant—women, like the Samaritan woman, Mary and Martha, and Mary Magdalene. These new figures press into the foreground and enlarge the circle of apostles. That is to say, they eliminate the theological significance of the apostles as a unique group. The memory of the historical past is not eradicated, but it is weakened into a typical pattern. The disciples who receive commission, Spirit and authority from the risen Christ are simply the representatives of the Christian community. In this community, each one is commissioned by being called to discipleship as narrated in John 1.41ff. and confirmed in 17.18ff. Unmistakably, John represents a Christianity in which ministerial functions are not yet connected with privileges. As in Paul, so here, the priesthood of all believers[6] is maintained, which is rather surprising at the end of

---

[4] Cf. A. Kragerud, *Der Lieblingsjünger im Johannesevangelium* (1959), pp. 53ff., 68ff.

[5] Barrett, *op. cit.*, pp. 79ff.; F. Mussner, 'Die johanneischen Parakletsprüche und die apostolische Tradition', *Biblische Zeitschrift*, 5 (1961), pp. 76f.; R. Schnackenburg, *Die Kirche im Neuen Testament* (1961), p. 30 (ET *The Church in the New Testament* [1965], p. 31).

[6] E. Hirsch, *op. cit.*, pp. 114, 346, 451; E. Schweizer, *op. cit.*, p. 373 (ET, pp. 237ff.).

the first century.[7] For John this doctrine is even more self-evident than for Paul, whose doctrine of differentiated charismata clearly indicates that the apostle was quite familiar with the problems contained in such a view. When John 3.34 engages in polemics against the Jewish arguments that the Spirit is always received only 'by measure', we have a clear indication that he is not at all interested in a differentiation of the gifts of the Spirit as the basis of a church order. There is no other writing in the whole New Testament of which this can be said. Was there ever a time when the Church was not troubled by questions of its order? In post-apostolic times, the problem of the Church's order moves into the foreground everywhere. Where is the situation, the locale, in which, at the end of the first century, one can be untouched by a problem like that? In view of this difficulty, it is understandable that the authority of the apostles is read into this Gospel, too. At any rate, this is more comprehensible than ignoring the difficulty altogether and locating the Johannine community, like a phantom, between heaven and earth. No church can be that invisible, not even the one from which the theological notion of the invisible Church may be deduced. If the apostles are honoured only as the first disciples retained in the memory of the historical past, then it must be possible to find a different kind of community structure which would agree with that outlook, a structure which would explain the seemingly anachronistic disinterest in forms of ecclesiastical organization. And indeed John does give us an indication, when again in an astonishing and to some degree anachronistic fashion he persistently calls the Christians 'disciples' and in so doing takes up the earliest Christian self-designation and employs it as a substitute for all ecclesiological titles. The expression 'the disciples' is, to be sure, part of the tradition. Its stereotyped use, however, makes it clear that the expression is taken up thoughtfully and deliberately and that it is meant to characterize the nature of the Johannine community at its very core. The verbs connected with this expression demonstrate that the aspects of hearing, learning, serving and following after are contained in it. In short, it really refers to 'the pupil'. Therefore, Jesus himself can be designated teacher, even though this designation falls short of the ideas contained in the title 'Son of God' in the Gospel. The self-understanding of the Johannine community inevitably produces far-reaching consequences. On the basis of this self-understanding in terms of 'the disciples', it becomes

7 Kragerud, op. cit., p. 64.

evident that the community is viewed primarily not from the aspect of its corporateness, but rather from the aspect of its individual members, while the general trend of later times is to incorporate the individual into the realm of the Church by organizational, sacramental and cultic means. The disciples are addressed from a peculiar esoteric aspect as 'friends'[8] in John 15.14f., and III John 15 shows that this address is used as the most intimate self-designation of the 'brethren' among themselves. If all are disciples, brothers, and friends of Jesus, then differentiations among them can no longer be decisive. The relationship to the Lord determines the whole picture of the Johannine Church to such an extent that the differences between individuals recede, and even the apostles represent only the historical beginnings of the community. Perhaps the most interesting feature in this connection is the role in the Gospel of John of women who are presented quite emphatically, like Mary Magdalene, as witnesses of the Easter event, or, like the Samaritan woman, as servants in the ministry of the proclamation of the Word. Paul had already expressed his veto against active participation of women in the worship of the community in I Cor. 14.34ff., even though women were used by him and in the succeeding periods for ministering to various needs and probably also for mission work within the women's quarter. But only heretical circles in the later strata of the New Testament entrusted the public proclamation or even the leadership within the community to women. The candour and frankness with which John in this instance swims against the stream characterizes his historical position.[9] Again we recognize him standing in the enthusiastic tradition, whose slogan and battle-cry is: 'There is neither male nor female.' In Corinth the most daring consequences had already been drawn from this slogan and as a result the later Church, which claimed the apostles as its foundation, retreated from any notion of Spirit-effected emancipation of women while, on the other hand, the heretics continued the older tradition.

If we review our investigation thus far from this aspect, our individual observations can be assembled into a picture. The community which knows itself to be governed by the Spirit can let the apostolate, the ministry and its organization melt into the background and

[8] Gaugler, *op. cit.*, p. 29, correctly called attention to the fact that in later times only mystical circles used this predication to indicate that personal fellowship with Christ determines them. It is no less significant that the 'friends' understand themselves as free men. Cf. Bultmann, *Evangelium*, p. 418.

[9] Hirsch, *op. cit.*, p. 305.

understand itself in the manner of a conventicle which is constituted through its individual members and which designates itself as the circle of friends and brothers. This community may take up and use the oldest self-designations and traditions of primitive Christianity, traditions which at the end of the first century appear outdated and obsolete, and thus come into conflict with developing early Catholicism. In short, John stands within an area of tensions in the Church.

His situation is also expressed in his understanding of cultic matters, especially the sacraments. The spirited controversy about John's relationship to the sacraments may perhaps at this moment have exhausted the argumentation on the basis of detailed exegetical analysis. It appears highly unlikely that the most extreme positions will permanently prevail.[10] Worship and sacraments do not play a dominant role in our Gospel.[11] On the other hand, however, there is no reason to assign all references to the sacraments to a redactor.[12] To be sure, the presence of redactional work in John may be demonstrated from chapter 21 and can hardly be denied for texts such as 6.51b–58. Yet undoubtedly the Evangelist not only knew of Jesus' baptism, but also presupposed the practice of Christian baptism and of the Lord's Supper in his community. If there are allusions to the sacraments in John 3.3ff.; 6.32ff. and in other texts, they are hardly surprising at the end of the first century. On the contrary, one would expect to find a multitude of sacramental allusions in a Christian document of that time. But it is not proper to read our expectations into the text of John, so long as a non-sacramental interpretation is possible. We gain nothing if we indulge in eisegesis, but only magnify the Johannine enigma at this very point. We must ask: Why does the same John who, as we are told, continuously indulges in sacramental allusions, and who, as we are ready to admit, did indeed presuppose the practice of the sacraments in the Christian community, nevertheless not narrate the institution of the sacraments? Why does he substitute the narrative of the foot-washing for the words of institution

[10] Compare H. Köster, 'Geschichte und Kultus im Johannesevangelium und bei Ignatius von Antiochien', *ZThK* 54 (1957), pp. 56–69 (ET 'History and Cult in the Gospel of John and in Ignatius of Antioch', *JThC* [1965], pp. 111–23); E. Lohse, 'Wort und Sakrament im Johannesevangelium', *NTS* 7 (1960), pp. 110–25.
[11] Contrary to Cullmann, *op. cit.*, p. 38 (ET, p. 37); W. Wilckens, *Die Entstehungsgeschichte des vierten Evangeliums* (1958); also Barrett, *op. cit.*, p. 69.
[12] Contrary to Bultmann.

of the Lord's Supper? Apparently this did not happen by accident, but rather by design. The *disciplina arcani*,[13] the endeavour to protect the sacredness of the Eucharist and eucharistic words from profanation would indeed explain the absence of the words of institution in John. However, it cannot be proven that this discipline already existed at that time.[14] Above all, those secrets in which John himself is truly interested are unfolded in wide-ranging monologues in the form of the secret discourse. Apart from 6.51b–58, there are no such monologues about baptism and the Lord's Supper. The theme of 3.3ff.; 6.32ff.; 15.1ff. is not the sacrament as such. On the other hand, we find in John many rather primitively constructed narratives which serve the Evangelist as points of departure for his own thoughts. Important features of primitive Christian faith and life and central contents of the primitive Christian proclamation are silently passed by in John, as a comparison with the Synoptic Gospels and with Paul reveals. This implies that the peculiar relationship of our Gospel to the sacraments and the cult may not be investigated and determined in isolation. It is rather a characteristic aspect within the total context of John's relationship to the earlier tradition. Simple and extreme solutions do not do justice to the problem of the use of tradition in John, which is quite complicated and should be approached dialectically. The exegetical controversy about the meaning of particular details, verses and sections cannot come to an end so long as the exegete endeavours to overcome the dialectics inherent in John by emphasizing either one or the other side of this Gospel.

The debate really centres upon John's conception of history, within the context of his doctrine of the incarnation. This is recognized by almost everyone, since everyone brings the problems of the Church, the ministry, the sacraments and tradition in John more or less clearly into relation with his doctrine of the incarnation, so that these problems are answered on this basis. Unfortunately most interpreters usually do not sufficiently consider the consequences of this kind of approach. For if the incarnation is really the pivotal point of all the problems under consideration here, then at this point, too, the primacy of christology has come to the fore, that christology which is the unmistakable feature of John's theology. Christology and history cannot simply be co-ordinated in this Gospel as though they were

---

[13] So J. Jeremias, *Die Abendmahlsworte Jesu*, 3rd ed. (1960), pp. 119ff. (ET *The Eucharistic Words of Jesus* [1966], pp. 125ff.).

[14] Lohse, *op. cit.*, p. 122.

more or less independent entities which can be brought together, placed side by side or separated. Still more important, christology may not be injected into history as though it were an eschatological novelty and history could be known without it. Incarnation is not merely a miraculous event within history. Incarnation rather means, as the prologue unmistakably indicates, the encounter of the Creator with his creature. This, however, implies that history and the world must be understood in this light and from this perspective. Without it, they cannot be understood at all. It is exactly this idea that is demonstrated by John on every single page of his Gospel. However, if this is so, then we pose the wrong questions when we investigate the significance of history in John without taking this aspect into consideration, or when we carry our historicist, existentialist or 'saving-historical' notions and conceptions into the Gospel. Of course, we cannot stop others from doing that, and, as a point of departure, even the raising of false questions may be fruitful. It should, however, be recognized that the premises in this case contain the problem and that the results at best reveal only part of the dialectical truth, and cannot do justice to all the Evangelist's intention. In the confrontation with the Creator, history ceases to be what we imagined it to be. John placed this idea at the very centre of his presentation and developed it with many variations. This idea is the perspective from which he composed his Gospel and therefore it is the hermeneutical key to its interpretation. This idea produced the dialectic which we must now develop in detail.

The statement 'The light shines in the darkness' does not differ basically from the statement 'The Word became flesh.'[15] The first sentence declares what becomes of the world as it encounters its Creator. This encounter reveals the world's whole past, present and future as darkness, in so far as it does not enter into and remain in the brilliant stream of light. The Gospel, therefore, describes the world as the realm of deficiencies and defects, of sickness and death, of lies, unbelief and misunderstanding, of doubts and sheer malice. This it is, perhaps more distinctly than anywhere else in its religious sphere, which in John is represented through Judaism. Because of this situation, the characteristic feature of this world cannot be a history which arranges the world's epochs and signifies its immanent path. The world has 'fathers' to which it appeals. Yet for the world, its fathers are only the projections of its own attitude into the past, just

15 Compare Käsemann, *op. cit.*, pp. 161f.

as Christ projects this attitude metaphysically into the work and sphere of the devil. The end of the world is, therefore, always present in death, appearing in many different forms and faces. Historicity is not really an attribute of the world as such. Historicity is present where the Creator acts in and on the world. Only God, in manifesting himself, truly brings about history, just as he alone can give life.

This statement that only revelation produces history must be put more precisely. It is characteristic of John that he refers to the creation of the world only in traditional formulae, except in the prologue. He does not mention Adam's fall at all and when he deals with Old Testament figures, which happens rather seldom, he does so in a manner which leaves them without clear historical features. Like John the Baptist, they are mentioned only in their function as witnesses of Jesus. We also occasionally find traditional formulae which speak of the general resurrection of the dead as the goal of history. Yet in these instances we may be dealing with later interpolations. Finally, only the traditional miracle stories which John took up depict individual persons in vivid colours. All other figures lack individuality and distinct features, because they characterize, from a functional viewpoint, the attitude and response of the world or of the Christian community to the encountered revelation.[16] In view of these facts, to interpret John in terms of salvation history is indeed more than risky, and permissible only if this kind of salvation history is clearly distinguished from other types such as the Pauline or the Lucan salvation history.[17] Of course, one can reduce the most diverse things to their lowest common denominator, provided one harmonizes, formalizes and ignores the differences. The task of exegesis, however, demands the bringing out of different emphases and distinct profiles. The Johannine salvation history is, to be precise, in its very essence the history of the Logos who overcomes or increases the world's resistance to its Creator. The fact that this resistance and its conquest are always depicted in typical scenes is further evidence that John's whole emphasis falls upon the revelation as such. The history narrated in his Gospel happens, to be sure, on earth, that is to say within time and space, and the Logos therefore requires human opponents and human partners. Apart from the traditional material, the reality of the Logos' opponents and partners is limited to the

[16] This is shown in principle, if somewhat exaggeratedly, by A. Loisy, *Le quatrième Évangile* (1921).

[17] Cf. Cullmann's interpretation.

function of reacting. Thus they can disappear as suddenly and abruptly as they appeared. They are 'drawn' either from below or from above and they act almost like puppets in the blindness of their foolishness. The light from above, falling upon them, puts them in motion, and only in the circle of this light do they have life. Thus, the history represented here can be regarded as a process only in the most external and superficial sense. Jesus is pictured as the one who is on the way and this picture is repeated on a higher level, since his way on earth is simultaneously his way back from the earth *via* the cross to heaven. The dimension of the past is retained only in so far as it points forward to his presence; all of the future is nothing but the glorified extension and repetition of this presence. History remains the history of the Logos, since it is the sphere of his past, present and future epiphany. The sole theme of history is the *praesentia Christi*. What else may happen on earth is only scenery and props for this theme. These earthly events are in part only intimated or roughly sketched, so that some narratives recede into twilight. Dogmatic reflection determines the structure and the subdivisions within this Gospel. Consequently the place of events can time and again be Jerusalem. Many of the traditions important to the Synoptics are uninteresting to John. The cleansing of the temple can be moved to the beginning, and the miracle of Lazarus' resurrection opens the passion story. The narrative material is used to illustrate Jesus' words and to introduce the long monologues of his discourses. Compared with the reality of everyday life, all of this is quite artificial.

If we keep this in mind, then John's relationship to the tradition as a whole also becomes intelligible. An evangelist who desires to narrate Jesus' earthly history cannot, as a matter of course, dispense with traditions. More astonishing is the fact that John, living at the end of the first century and situated, it would seem, not too far from Palestine, possibly in Syria, in all probability does not know the Synoptics themselves, but rather a tradition whose purer and more original form is preserved in the Synoptics, and which is known to him in a version which has to some extent run wild. Again, this would point to a time and place in the history of primitive Christianity where the currents of the emerging early Catholic Church are not very strong. The peculiar feature of the Johannine use of tradition, however, is that he deals with what he has received more freely and more vigorously than anyone else in the New Testament. It would be false to argue that John is contemptuous of tradition, or that he engages in a basic criticism of tradition by contrasting the Spirit with tradition. If such a contrast was to have been drawn at any time in the history of primitive Christianity, then it would have had to be relatively soon after Easter, when, for instance, the circle around Stephen transgressed the Jewish cultic law for the sake of missionary work among the Gentiles, or when the Corinthian enthusiasts with their realized eschatology, based on the efficacy of the sacraments, broke up the traditional Jewish-Christian apocalyptic frame. John no longer belongs to this stage, even if certain roots of his do reach into the past. The alternative 'tradition or Spirit' is quite alien to his thought. For him, the Spirit calls the words of Jesus to mind and he himself actualizes that by writing a Gospel which in form and content has many parallels with the Synoptics. He did not despise the use of the Old Testament[18] even though he can get along without it in large sections and he always puts it into the shadow of his traditions about Jesus. He probably took over at least in part and without great modifications narratives from a source containing miracle stories, and the same is true with regard to the core of his passion and Easter accounts. With all of this, John discloses that tradition is absolutely necessary and that without tradition the Spirit becomes spiritual falsehood. Here again we recognize that it is not a matter of alternatives, but rather of shifts in emphases and perspectives. Such shifts can be seen in the fact that the voice of the Spirit is not limited to tradition and that the tradition is not, as stated in II Peter 1.12; 3.2; Jude 3, once and for all time fixed in the apostolic tradition. Jesus who comes again in the Spirit is identified through the tradition, but Jesus is more than tradition. His guidance into all truth cannot be separated from the tradition which witnesses to his work with his first disciples, but it is not exhausted by this tradition. For his work grows, and the glory of succeeding times is greater than that of the beginnings. Finally, we must take note that the tradition of the apostles is nowhere directly and unmistakably encountered as such. Wherever exegesis affirms the contrary,[19] it operates within the categories of fantasy. Just as the eleven represent the Christian community and beyond that have only historical significance, so their work and heritage is not basically differentiated from the work

[18] Compare N. A. Dahl, 'The Johannine Church and History', in: *Current Issues in New Testament Interpretation. Essays in Honor of O. A. Piper* (1962), pp. 124–42.

[19] A representative of this view is Mussner, *op. cit.*, pp. 66ff.

of the Samaritan woman or the work of later times, for instance in the case of the Hellenists in 12.20ff. The sole qualification of genuine tradition is that the voice of Jesus is contained in it. Tradition is not an end in itself, but the means of the witness which is legitimated neither through the name and rank of the witness-bearers, but through its content and object. If tradition has but this sole function —namely, to retain Jesus' voice, then it is at the same time limited and relativized by this function. The voice of Jesus, which is to lead the community ever anew into all truth, can never have tradition as its substitute. On the contrary, the primitive Christian tradition stands under the same motto as everything that is earthly: 'It is the Spirit which makes alive, the flesh is of no avail.' Whatever does not serve as a witness for Christ is cast away, regardless of how important it may have been historically. Even the tradition which is acknowledged is ruthlessly moved into new contexts, as the whole Gospel proves, because it is not the past which sanctions and legitimates a tradition, but rather its possible usage in the present. It is not at all sufficiently emphasized that John must be seen in the historical and theological context of a Christian prophecy whose characteristic feature, according to I Cor. 14, is the actualization of the Christian proclamation.[20] Just as this prophecy is determined by the particular situation as it teaches, admonishes, rebukes, comforts and interprets anew the tradition to its own time, so likewise John carried the Gospel with prophetic ruthlessness and one-sidedness into his present situation, using as much or as little of the tradition as suited his purpose. In John, polemic is more than merely a literary device for his speeches.[21] The prophet must discern the spirits. This also includes the repudiation of what is antiquated in order to remain faithful to the one who abides. Zinzendorf's confession also holds true for John: 'I have but one passion. That is He, and only He.' Obvious as it may appear to us, such a confession was precisely what was not self-evident in the history of Christianity. It rather marks the important exceptions, and quite frequently it points to a sectarian type of piety. While such a confession does not necessarily imply a criticism of the received tradition, it can easily lead to that. Above all, it preserves the Lord's freedom over against the ecclesiastical tradition.

We have to pause here for a moment and voice our opinion that

[20] Kragerud, op. cit., p. 114, has seen that, even though I cannot otherwise agree with his analysis.
[21] Barrett, op. cit., pp. 11f.; Mussner, op. cit., p. 64; Brown, op. cit., p. LXXVIII.

these observations indicate the historical situation in which this Gospel arose. If it more or less clearly presupposes the conditions and trends at the end of the first century, even if its own concerns and purposes do not easily accord with those conditions and trends, then the Gospel would fit best into a side tributary apart from the general stream yet connected with it. The fact that only occasional glances are cast in the direction of the Church's situation and that many points at issue run counter to it should be interpreted as polemic on the part of John. Does the key to the problem of the seeming lack of a historical context and of the other-worldly quality of this Gospel, which has puzzled all church history, actually lie in the explanation that the Fourth Gospel did not grow up within the realm of the Church known to us through the New Testament, the Church on which all John's interpreters focus their attention? Of course, no universal church organization existed at the end of the first century. The independence of the communities and the differences of their conditions and expressions can hardly be exaggerated. Yet in spite of all the differences, the independent and divergent communities were pressing toward unity and did so in various ways, with varying clarity of purpose and varying degrees of speed. Paul had already endeavoured to manifest unity. The Book of Acts and the Letter to the Ephesians draw up a theological programme for it. The formation of the New Testament canon was possible only because the Christian past was seen naïvely and perhaps even ideologically in the light of this trend toward unity. Finally, the progress in the formation of the Catholic Church is clear up to the middle of the second century. If the Fourth Gospel fits least well into this development and is first discovered by the gnostics, then the reason for this may be that John is the relic of a Christian conventicle existing on, or being pushed to, the Church's periphery. The historian at least may not discard this possibility, even though it contradicts the high esteem in which our Gospel has always been held in the history of the Church, and may cause difficulty for the theologian. Historical scholarship always has disillusioning and demythologizing results. We have seen how our assumption of John's historical position throws light upon his christology. The difficulties of his ecclesiology and the peculiar dialectical relation to tradition can also be more thoroughly understood on the basis of our assumption. The man who lives on the fringe of the prevailing development of the Church can oppose its trends and simultaneously be subjected to them, as his very reaction shows. Turning to the past, he can take up old traditions and at the same time prepare the way for new developments, provided his reaction is not sterile, but fruitful. By contradicting the present in his faithfulness toward the past, he is already contributing to the scaffolding of the future. Sectarians also participated in the formation of the early Catholic Church and they were more influential than orthodoxy was at any time willing to admit. Admission to the canon means the acknowledgment of a writing, not of the atmosphere and environment in which it grew up. The productive and the unproductive errors are likewise part of a realistically understood history of salvation under God's providence.

It would be foolish to deny that obviously John also sets out an ecclesiology. But his ecclesiology is not designed on the basis of the forms of church organizations. As a result, the institution as such is not glorified by means of that mythology which is abundantly present in John's christological thought. For John, the Church is basically and exclusively the fellowship of people who hear Jesus' word and believe in him; in short, it is the community under the Word.[22] All other ecclesiological definitions are oriented on this one and significant only in so far as they give expression to it. But this also means that the Church is viewed here with strange emphasis from the perspective of its individual members. To hear, to believe and to follow is something that only the individual himself and not his representative can and must do, even if he does it within the Christian brotherhood. Pointedly, but not exaggeratedly, we take note that John, as the first theologian, passionately rejects the principle that it is sufficient to believe with the Church and to be supported by the Church as the mother of the individual. John, therefore, could not base salvation upon the tradition as such. Tradition calls attention to Jesus, and in this respect it is indispensable. But tradition remains fundamentally misunderstood when it does not instruct one's own faith. Tradition always remains dangerous because of its tendency to pass itself off as the voice of the Good Shepherd and to drown his voice. Our relationship to Jesus cannot be moved into the historical dimension and be made dependent on our relation to the Church, even though the voice of the Good Shepherd is heard in the Church and transmitted by it. The voice of the Good Shepherd is not qualified or limited by the Church's transmission, nor does his voice receive its authority from tradition. It is his voice which qualifies, limits and empowers the

---

[22] Most strongly emphasized by A. Schlatter, *Der Evangelist Johannes* (1948), and R. Bultmann.

Church as the community under the Word. Thus John 4.39, certainly not without polemical intentions, denies the idea that the mere witness of faith transmitted only by men creates a sufficient relationship to Jesus.[23] The mark of true faith, according to John, is that a man has himself seen and heard Jesus and is following him. Otherwise one would still be in the situation of the Jews who hold on to the faith and the traditions of their fathers and in this very way close their hearts against Christ.

Of course, the question now arises how, after Jesus' death, it is still possible to see and hear for oneself and in this sense to be the Church. The answer is given pointedly, in that Thomas is challenged to a faith which has not seen. The answer is not really paradoxical, because Thomas had indeed seen before and the farewell discourses in 14.7ff.; 16.16ff.; and 17.24 promise the disciples that they shall also see in the future. It is therefore not the case that two stages are contrasted, the first determined by seeing, the second by not seeing. Rather, John's call to believe without having seen clearly indicates that for John the object of seeing is not the historical Jesus as we call him.[24] The promise of seeing Jesus even after his exaltation establishes that the faith of later generations is not dependent to such a degree on the Church's proclamation as assent to dogmatic propositions would have to be. True faith goes beyond the mere word of men, even though it be the word of Spirit-filled men and of the Church. Even if after Easter faith can arise only on the basis of the Church's proclamation, faith must still come to Jesus himself, just as the Samaritans had to meet him directly after the woman's proclamation. Faith is thus guarded against misunderstanding on two sides. For John, faith is neither *fides historica* nor *fides dogmatica*. But how can this be maintained, when on one hand faith has already been evoked by the historical Jesus, having him as its object and content, and when, on the other, as shown earlier, it is none other than John who determines the nature of faith dogmatically, that is, as faith in Jesus' divine Sonship, and when all post-Easter faith arises only on the basis of such dogmatically oriented proclamation? It is one of the most important tasks of Johannine interpretation to raise this problem and to answer it exactly. One can hardly affirm that recent

[23] Compare Bultmann, *Evangelium*, pp. 148f.; Hirsch, *op. cit.*, p. 153; R. Walker, 'Jüngerwort und Herrenwort', *ZNW* 57 (1966), pp. 49–54, is not convincing.
[24] Contrary to Cullmann, *op. cit.*, p. 112 (ET, p. 115); Barrett, *op. cit.*, p. 72.

interpretation has advanced very far at this point. In general, it has suppressed either the one side or the other, and thus missed the dilemma which confronts us here. Modern Johannine scholarship had to argue in one-sided fashion because it was fascinated either by the notion of the incarnation or by John's supposed spirituality and as a result interpreted the christology accordingly. Here it becomes evident that John's christology may not be interpreted on the basis of our ideas about the nature of incarnation or about his supposed spirituality, but on the contrary, incarnation and what is commonly called spirituality or mysticism must be understood in the light of his christology. His christology alone finally determines whether the problems of our Gospel have really been recognized and properly solved. Neither is the case when, as is customary, the alternative of humiliation and exaltation with its patterns becomes the interpretative key. For the Logos who is one with the Father is encountered also in the earthly Jesus, and the Church's post-Easter proclamation has but one purpose, namely the encounter with the Logos. In the encounter with the earthly Jesus and in the post-Easter proclamation, the object and content of faith remain identical, namely, the revealer who as Logos is one with the Father. The communication of historical facts legitimated through the eye-witness accounts of apostles does not profit at all as such,[25] just as the earthly Jesus himself was met with more unbelief than faith in spite of all his miracles. Likewise, the dogmatic proclamation of the Church profits nothing as such unless it opens the path to Jesus himself. Dogmatic proclamation as such could substantiate merely one religion with specific saving facts among other religions. Conversely, Jesus drew near to us on earth and he also wills to come to us on earth in the Spirit. While on earth, he already cast his message in dogmatic form as the message of his divine Sonship. Thus the Church cannot surrender the dogmatic commitment in its own proclamation, because otherwise the Church would not take up Jesus' proclamation. The encounter on earth and obligation to the dogma belong together, both before and after Easter. They belong together, in so far as both are held together by and subsumed under the concept of 'witness'. Witness in John is a strictly forensic concept, presupposing the situation of legal proceedings.[26] The earthly Jesus himself is no less 'witness' than the Spirit

---

[25] Contrary to Cullmann, *op. cit.*, p. 48 (ET, pp. 47f.).
[26] So already Heitmüller, *op. cit.*, p. 16; Dahl, *op. cit.*, pp. 139f.; also Bultmann, *passim*.

who speaks in and through the post-Easter Church, or the fathers of the Old Testament who testified before the incarnation and John the Baptist. It is very important to note that Jesus unceasingly opposes the idea of bearing witness merely for himself and thus seeking his own glory. But he also opposes the idea that the voices of the Baptist or of the fathers of the Old Testament are to be regarded as the final court of appeal. As witnesses they point beyond themselves. The dogmatic proclamation of the post-Easter church likewise points beyond itself. Were it not dogmatic, then it would not do justice to Jesus' claim to divine Sonship. If it did not point beyond itself, it would not lead to Jesus himself. If this is so, then the earthly Jesus as witness must also point beyond himself, to the Father. Thus the truth can never be imprisoned and objectified in any earthly object as such, not even in the earthly Jesus, whom, with the intention of objectifying, we call the historical Jesus. His dignity is to be the Logos and his claim is that by means of all Logoi one can come to the Logos himself. In the Son, but also in the message of the fathers or in the Church's tradition, the Father will and must be known. And according to 17.3, only through this knowledge can one gain eternal life.

To summarize the results thus far: the witness of the fathers, the word and work of the earthly Jesus and the dogmatic proclamation of the Church are the historical aspects of the one and unvarying revelation of the Logos who is one with the Father. These aspects each have their own peculiar function. They indicate the dimensions of the revelation in its depth reaching back to creation, in its nearness as salvation and in its world-wide scope. As historical aspects of the revelation, they are also subject to the same danger of misunderstanding, that is, that their earthly appearance blocks the access to the heavenly truth manifesting itself in them. Just as the Old Testament fathers can become the court of appeal against Christ and the Church's proclamation again and again threatens to replace Christ, so likewise the claim of the earthly Jesus based on his incarnation becomes unbelievable to some and to others the occasion for temptation by dreams of earthly materialistic salvation. Even the incarnation stands in the twilight and in conflict which is overcome only by that faith which perceives the glory of Jesus and all glory only in Jesus. The revelation of the Logos is the meaning and the criterion of the incarnation, not *vice versa*, as if the incarnation were the truth, the confines and limits of the Logos. The Logos determines the function of the incarnation just as he determines the function of the witness of the fathers and of the Church's tradition. They all serve his presence, but his presence cannot be detained in any one of them forever. For history is the sphere of revelation and the earthly reality is the shape of the epiphany of revelation, but history and the earthly reality are at the same time the realm of his pilgrimage. They do not and cannot guarantee that he remains, for they do not have power over him whom the Father has sent and who himself sends the Spirit when, where and how it pleases him. In the historical and earthly sphere of this world, his works and signs are erected, but his kingdom is not of this world. When this is understood then the Church's worship and the sacraments also receive their proper place. They also point beyond themselves. Everything depends on remaining with Jesus himself and remaining under his Word. Therefore the sacraments are oriented towards the Word and his epiphany, and are interpreted in the light of the Word. The truth of the sacraments is the lordship of the Word. Apart from this insight the sacraments are not dealt with.

The customary interpretation of John emphasizes the sacraments and their significance for the Fourth Gospel, because the incarnation is understood in the light of the sacrament. The incarnation is then interpreted within the context of the so-called anti-docetic realism of this Gospel.[27] However, the Johannine trend runs in the very opposite direction. Just as John does not regard the Church as the institution of salvation, so he does not give a picture of the so-called historical Jesus. Not even the Synoptics had given one, though historicizing tendencies can be shown to be present in them. Apart from material which was transmitted to John by his tradition, namely the traditional miracle stories and the passion tradition, John's supposed realism can be based only on the statement in 1.14a, as is usually unhesitatingly done by the customary interpretation. The fact that incarnation does not have to mean kenosis (Phil. 2.7), total entering into our humanity, is rarely even considered and, if so, generally rejected. It then appears insignificant that the Johannine Christ says to his mother, 'Woman, what have I to do with you?', that he confronts all his disciples and all his opponents as the incomparable and unique one. It also appears insignificant, or else it is overlooked, that John understands the sacraments as a possible encounter with the Logos and thus robs them of the kind of 'sacramental'

---

[27] Cullmann, op. cit., pp. 38f., 56f., 112 (ET, pp. 37f., 55f., 115); Hoskyns, op. cit., pp. 17f.; Barrett, op. cit., p. 69; Wilckens, op. cit., pp. 24, 91; quite carefully on the other hand, Brown, op. cit., pp. lxxvif., cxiff.

quality usually associated with them. Historical realism, in the period after the Enlightenment, has become one of the last bastions of Christianity, which now uses slogans that were originally hostile to Christianity and which understands the incarnation in a modern sense, that is, historically. Of course, John maintains that the encounter with the revealer took place in the earthly sphere and is still taking place there. Otherwise the encounter would become a religious dream and an illusion. But this does not mean that the revealer himself gives up his divinity and becomes as earthly as we are. Judged by the modern concept of reality, our Gospel is more fantastic than any other writing of the New Testament. We render poor service to John, and we can hardly deceive true realists, if we attach the label 'antidocetic' to John, to guarantee the 'once and for all historical event'.[28] Over against this the opposite slogans 'spiritualistic' and 'mystical' at least had heuristic significance, even though by themselves they are unusable and misleading. We take note that even in his ecclesiology John's naïve docetism which is not thought through nor elevated into dogma and which we had affirmed for his christology is continued.[29] It is for this very reason that neither the incarnation nor tradition, the historical past nor the sacraments possess the significance which modern interpreters assign to them and which we would expect them to exert at the end of the first century. For this reason, the Church is not yet regarded as the institution of salvation and history is viewed only as the place of the inbreaking of the Creator, not the realm in which he can become objectified and limited.

If the two magical formulae, 'historical realism' and 'mystical spiritualism', both fail in the same way, then we are left with that category which is already offered in the prologue, that is, the category of the Word. It is exclusively this category which dominates John's ecclesiology, thus expressing most succinctly that his ecclesiology is unfolded without any qualifications from his christology as the point of departure, namely from the Logos. As the Church is the community under the Word and as all characteristic features of the Church are related to the Word, so likewise the Spirit is related to the Word. In John, the Spirit is nothing else but the continual possibility and reality of the new encounter with Jesus in the post-Easter

---

[28] Contrary to Köster, *op. cit.*, p. 69 (ET, p. 123).
[29] Our argumentation thus far has not yet conclusively proved this point, as the analysis of Christ's relationship to the world and of the heavenly union will show. But at this earlier point I would like to prepare the way for my later thesis.

situation as the one who is revealing his Word to his own and through them to the world. For the first time in Christian history, the Spirit is bound exclusively to and dependent on the Word of Jesus. Paul had already moved in that direction when he no longer interpreted the Spirit primarily in terms of a miracle-producing and ecstasy-evoking supernatural power. For Paul, the exalted Christ is manifest on earth in the proclamation and this manifestation is mediated by the Spirit. Therefore, antithetically, Paul can argue in I Cor. 12.2 that the idolaters were moved by dumb spirits. But the final step was not taken by Paul. For him, the Word remains the means and effect of the Spirit, but the Spirit itself remains the heavenly power manifesting itself also in miracles and ecstasies. John, however, identified the Spirit with the voice of Jesus which in the form of the Paraclete continues to speak from heaven to the disciples when he himself is no longer with them. Only in his Word is the heavenly Christ still accessible, just as the power of the resurrection and therefore the Spirit bring the Gospel ever anew into the community. The watchword of the earthly Jesus was: 'Abide with me, that is, in my Word', and this continues to be the sole watchword for the Christian and for Christianity after Jesus' death. Discipleship means to remain with him. Since time, space and life incessantly change, therefore discipleship is possible only when the prophetic Word is heard ever anew. Abiding with Jesus is possible only in the pilgrimage on that way which is Jesus himself. The same subject, the prophetic Word, is stated in II Peter 1.19, but there it deals with the prophecy which is enclosed in the Bible, proclaimed by prophets, and interpreted by the Church as the final court of doctrinal decisions. The difference from John is self-evident. In radical reduction John made Jesus and his witness into the sole content and criterion of the true tradition of the Spirit. In so doing he retained the living voice of prophecy at a time when otherwise it had already receded or disappeared, a time when the sound doctrine of a developing orthodoxy and the edifying historicizing report became important. For John, Jesus himself is the continuity of the Christian community in all ages, whose other qualities must be judged from there. In John salvation history is Jesus' history, communicated and sustained by the Word which unites all generations. It is not its tradition as such, not even its love toward Jesus and certainly not its organization which unites the Church, but the Word of Jesus alone, his electing, sanctifying and uniting Word. Therefore hearing, listening, is the outstanding feature of this community and no other criterion may replace it or over-shadow it. Those who hear Jesus' Word and follow him, the disciples, are the beloved, the friends, the elect. Only the Word which is heard can save and preserve. The confirmation of this interpretation lies in John's viewpoint of the world as the antagonist of the Church. The world, for John, is that which desires miracles but closes its ears to the Word of Jesus. Faith and sin, salvation and condemnation, part company on Jesus' Word and are also determined by Jesus' Word. Perhaps for this reason the Jews are regarded as the representatives of the world. They have not only been the opponents of the earthly Jesus, as a later Gentile Christian point of view would argue, fore-shortening and schematizing historical facts at this point also. For John, the Jews are also the representatives of the religious tradition, so that the problem of hearing—of being unwilling to hear and unable to hear—could best be exemplified in them.

This, however, raises an important and difficult problem. Every-thing said thus far remains meaningless if this Word of Jesus is with-out definite content. There would be sheer anarchy if Jesus' Word were controlled only by the prophetic Spirit and the particular historical situation. The earliest communities soon came to know that the prophets rarely agree when left to themselves. And, in general, the ever-changing historical situations are not so unambi-guous that the commandment to love God and one's neighbour would suffice, even apart from the consideration that this 'great command-ment' itself does not have to be understood within a Christian con-text. The apocalyptic visionaries are not the only ones who have to ask, 'What does the Spirit say to the churches?' Does not this Gospel, too, leave us completely in the lurch?

At first glance it certainly appears that John teaches nothing 'specific or concrete',[30] no particular doctrine.[31] Johannine inter-pretation has tried to solve this in various ways. Some scholars have even gone so far as to dissolve the 'word-character' of the Johannine Logos and to substitute a particular content[32] or else, in opposition to

[30] Bultmann, *Theologie*, p. 414 (ET II, p. 62).
[31] Bultmann, *Theologie*, p. 415 (ET II, p. 63). Bultmann, *Evangelium*, p. 42; Hirsch, *op. cit.*, p. 269.
[32] Dodd, *Interpretation*, p. 330, speaks of God's self-disclosure in the broadest possible sense, even in the silent operation within the mind of man; Hirsch, *op. cit.*, p. 269, speaks of the power of love which . . . changes heart and conscience; Gaugler, *op. cit.*, pp. 185f., speaks of mystical, and Cullmann, *op. cit.*, p. 109 (ET, p. 113), of eucharistic communion.

this kind of solution, they have simply emphasized the actual utterance of the word as being of sole importance.[33] In Bultmann's formulation the 'that', the fact that there is a word spoken, has displaced the 'what', the content of the word.[34] This alternative is the means by which Bultmann interprets the peculiar phenomenon, that the Johannine Christ always and everywhere proclaims only himself as the divine revealer. At least modern Protestantism is no longer willing to understand the assertions of the Johannine Christ about himself in terms of dogmatic statements, say, within the context of the doctrine of the Trinity. Therefore, Protestants must necessarily make his assertions about himself into an abbreviation, a cipher, of the divine reality and love revealing itself there, or of the encounter with the divine claim taking place ever anew in Christian preaching. In the first case, the Johannine mythology can be understood as the symbolic expression of a metaphysical truth; in the second case, the Johannine mythology is regarded as an ancient form which is meant to express the fact that the demand for decisions is inherent in the divine call which results in life or death.[35] It follows that in the first case faith is described in experiential categories as 'turning toward the *eschaton* through faithful believing'[36] or as a form of vision,[37] while in the second, faith is described from the existentialist viewpoint in formal categories as the ever-new 'overcoming of the offence'.[38] The dilemma of an interpretation which moves in extreme alternatives should already prompt us to ask whether modern premises and assumptions have not been read into the text. Does the Johannine mythology really have only a symbolic significance, so that it indicates either a particular idea of God and a particular understanding of the world resulting from that idea or the importance of the situation of decision? Is this sort of demythologizing really conceivable anywhere in primitive Christianity of the first century? If we answer in the negative, then evidently we have no other possibility except to give up the modern premises, that John or his tradition were incapable of saying what they really wanted to say, or that the Johannine mythology was not meant to be taken literally by them, or that it could not be an early form of dogmatic statements.

[33] Bultmann, *Evangelium*, p. 432; *Theologie*, p. 416 (ET II, p. 63).
[34] Bultmann, *Theologie*, pp. 419f. (ET II, pp. 66f.).
[35] Bultmann, *Theologie*, pp. 414f. (ET II, p. 62).
[36] Faulhaber, *op. cit.*, p. 32.
[37] Dodd, *Interpretation*, p. 186.
[38] Bultmann, *Theologie*, pp. 421ff., 428f. (ET II, pp. 68ff., 75f.)

The christological witness of the Fourth Gospel is meant and formulated in a thoroughly dogmatic manner. The witness of the glory of
Jesus, of his unity with the Father, in short, the witness of his divinity,
is really the content of the Johannine message. The communication
of content and the direct address are inseparable in John as they are
in the Synoptics.

But can this observation help us any further? This kind of dogmatic declaration about Jesus' divinity can be continuously repeated
and paraphrased with synonyms as is also done in John. But can
such a declaration also be unfolded prophetically, can it be actualized
in the ever-changing situations through admonition, judgment,
comfort and teaching? In short, can such dogmatic declaration be
used as *kerygma*? A Protestantism which has ceased to be oriented to
dogma will have to ask questions such as these. The alternatives in
modern Johannine interpretation did not arise by accident, but
resulted from the attempt at translation which produced the two
most extreme possibilities. Is there a middle-of-the-road approach
which the Gospel itself indicates? We shall have to consider the
remarkable feat which distinguishes the Word, in the singular, from
the words of Jesus, without wanting to separate the two. For the
singular use does not designate the sum total of the individual words,
their content or their meaning.[39] Instead, the Johannine parallelism
and identification of works and words must be taken into account.[40]
The words of Jesus are simply the ever-new proclamation of the one
Word, which is Jesus himself, in different ways and circumstances. We
could boldly put it in this way: It is the interpretation of the Word
having become Spirit, through the Word becoming flesh entering a
specific time and space in the Christian proclamation. We do not
have this one Word in the multiplicity of different doctrines, nor in a
summa theologica, even if the one Word should produce these out of
itself, though John does not reflect on this. Nor do we have the one
Word in a multiplicity of ethical demands.[41] To be sure, the Fourth
Gospel does identify the words of Jesus with his commandments. But
they in turn are comprehended in the one demand, to remain with
Jesus in faith. The commandments make Jesus' claim concrete in
specific situations. Later, we shall show that the commandment of

---

[39] Contrary to Dodd, *Interpretation*, p. 266.
[40] Bultmann, *Theologie*, pp. 413f. (ET II, pp. 6of.).
[41] W. Bauer, *Johannesevangelium*, p. 191 on John 15.7ff., speaks of the moral
aspect of the relationship to Christ.

love does not negate this observation. The radical reduction of the whole theology to christology is also reflected in the terminological dialectic of Word, words, and commandments. We have the one Word, which is Jesus himself, only in the words of Christian preaching. We have the one Word—since the words of Christian preaching can be merely a witness—only if those words move us to come to Jesus himself and to remain with him in discipleship and under the lordship of the Word. At least we have now gained the insight that John knew the actualization of the witness of Jesus about himself to be both feasible and necessary in continually new situations. He could clothe his doctrine in the form of a Gospel, because in his view his doctrine was not merely the object of assent. Just as he would not separate doctrine from the *kerygma*, so he demanded that it must be kerygmatically developed.

We make some further progress when we recognize another terminological variation in John 17. The participation which Jesus granted his disciples in his glory is described in John 13 and 15 as a participation in his love. This motif is taken up in John 17 in terms of participation in the Word of God or of the revelation of the divine name. Apparently, Jesus' glory, his love, the revelation of the Word of God, of truth and of the divine name belong together and become interchangeable. They designate the same occurrence under different aspects, just as the formulae of Jesus' commission by the Father, the oneness with him and the election express different aspects of the same occurrence. We now must inquire about the reason, the hidden basis and purpose of this multiplicity of expressions. What all these various expressions have in common is that through them the activity of Jesus is described as the activity of God and *vice versa*, the work of God is designated as the work of Jesus. In Jesus, and only in him, we encounter God himself. He alone is the revealer. This is brought out most clearly when John employs the traditional expression of the revelation of the divine name. In antiquity, the name meant the manifestation of a being. Through its manifestation one can know and take hold of that being. The name of God is God himself as he manifests himself within the earthly realm. In his activity, Jesus proclaims, represents and brings God manifesting himself. Jesus is the one who is sent from heaven and as such, according to the rabbinical principle, he is like the sender himself, with the whole divine authority standing behind him.

This compels us to further inquiry. Who, according to our Gospel, is the God who is coming to earth in Jesus? The Johannine figurative discourses and 'I am' sayings give the answer when they refer to light, truth, life, heavenly bread and water, to those figures of speech of which Bultmann is the supreme interpreter—they speak of what enables man to live. In so doing they proclaim exclusiveness and absoluteness, by confronting his gift with the earthly possibilities. Earthly bread, life, water and light are at best the reflection and the sign of such a gift, but usually they become false substitutes for the heavenly possibility and reality. This means that only God is, and gives, life, light and truth, only he can satisfy hunger and thirst always and everywhere. He can do this as the Creator. If the nature and work are manifest in Jesus and if his commission, his authority and his own nature are to make God manifest, then we encounter the Creator in Jesus. He is the way, the truth and the life because he reveals the Father as the Creator and the Creator as the Father. He is God in his turning towards the world, and in this respect he is one with the Father, yet simultaneously our Lord, helper and friend. His glory, love and election are shown in that he brings the world back into the state of creation and that his Word, issuing forth ever again, calls us to remain the creation reborn. We have stated earlier that in our Gospel eschatology has turned into protology. Now we understand the reason and the necessity for this shift, namely, the last creation leads back to the first. The one who is the end also reveals the beginning, God himself who as the Creator is the father of his creature. What is stated in the primitive Christian hymns and confessions about Christ as mediator of creation is extended by John, with the radicalism typical of him, into man's everyday life. Paul had moved in the same direction when he regarded the new creature as the work of Christ and, conversely, John does not permit the eschatological aspect of the Pauline declaration to disappear, since for him the resurrection and eternal life are the gifts of Jesus. However, he does not give the eschatological aspects only a dimension of depth, which comprises world history up to creation. This was still possible for Paul, too, though for him it was more unusual. The real difference from Paul is indicated by the absence of a theology of the cross. For John, the cross is Jesus' victory over the world. Therefore the power of the resurrection is no longer expressed primarily in the fact that the community is willing and able to carry the cross and follow Jesus. The community is not spared temptation and suffering. They are no longer the eschatological birth-pangs through which the new creature is being born, but rather the pressure of a hostile environment. Consequently the future is not anticipated in the present through the preservation of the faith and urgent expectation, whereby the Spirit is the power of hope and the down-payment of glorification. The eschatological future in John only brings the final separation from the world, and with it the confirmation of the freedom now already granted. What is missing is the great Pauline paradox, that the power of the resurrection can be experienced only in the shadow of the cross, and that the reality of the resurrection now implies a position under the cross. The place of this paradox is taken by the dialectical declaration that no one can remain with Jesus unless he continually encounters him anew. One must be with him on the way, otherwise one cannot have him. In distinction from most other New Testament writers, John does not regard the world as an enticing, tempting power against which only the cross can protect. Christian existence is not, as in Paul, endangered by the flesh which signifies man's own worldliness. Accordingly our Gospel has no need of an explicit anthropology. The problem of the disciple's existence is not whether he actually reaches the goal, but rather whether he remains with Jesus. This is not, as so largely in the Synoptics, a question of the disciple's faithfulness, but rather of the preserving love of his Lord. The one who has created him through rebirth to eternal life must also preserve him. It is the glory of the parting Christ that he has lost no one except Judas, who was predestined by Scripture to perdition. As the Good Shepherd, Jesus protects his own, keeps them together and thus exhibits the omnipotence which the Father entrusted to him. No power can tear them out of his hands. He is the victor both in gathering and in preserving his community, whose existence is and remains the manifestation of his sole creative efficacy.

We realize that John, in distinction to the Corinthian enthusiasts, takes quite seriously the danger from the world which threatens the Christian and Christendom. He does not take the easy way and, like them, proclaim that freedom from temptation and inner turmoil is the result of receiving the sacraments. In John the community is exposed to satanic attacks. For this very reason the community is incapable of resisting through its own power and resources. The community remains the flock which the Good Shepherd must defend. Nevertheless John also proclaims the victory won over the community, and the basis for that is Christ's divinity. We shall have to interpret the miracle stories of this Gospel from this perspective, too. Beyond doubt, the miracles in John are primarily meant to be manifestations of the glory of Jesus. This point is brought out not only in the story of the wedding at Cana, but also in the account of the raising of Lazarus who has to lie in the grave for four days before Jesus intervenes. But the recognition of the manifestation of Jesus' glory in miracles should not mislead us into excluding completely the notion of divine help and mercy which is present at least in the healing narratives and in the story of the miraculous feeding. For John, that which is true is not contained in the earthly reality, for the earthly reality is at best the reflection of that which is heavenly. For this reason, all miracles remain signs pointing beyond themselves to the revelation occurring in the Logos himself. Nevertheless, for John the miracles are also 'proofs' of divine power in the sphere of the transitory.[42] They demonstrate the truth of the saying in 10.10, that Jesus came that his own might have life and have it abundantly. Such proofs are naturally ambiguous and, if isolated from the Logos, misleading, as the objections against the pre-Johannine miracle tradition indicate. Anyone who does not recognize and acknowledge the giver in the gifts and does not see the gifts as signs that lead to the giver himself exchanges the heavenly reality for the earthly and in so doing comes to naught. Conversely, the Logos drawing near to man does not designate himself only in terms of heavenly water, bread, light, life, truth and joy which are received through him, so that all depends on assent to this message. He also acts in such a way that even in the realm of the transitory, his Word is being confirmed and signs point and call attention to his true dignity. Even though these signs may confuse the world, in them his own disciples experience the presence of the Good Shepherd and the door to their pasture. The Word is not without signs.

In conclusion, we may summarize: John, with his message of the revealer who has come and who is one with the Father, places the community in the situation of which his first verses speak, in the situation of the beginning when the Word of God came forth and called the world out of darkness into light and life. This beginning is not a past occurrence in saving history, which is lost for ever. It is instead the new reality eschatologically revealed, which in the Christian community is disclosed every day and on earth through the Word and which every day and on earth must be received and

[42] Contrary to Hirsch, *op. cit.*, p. 124 and Haenchen, *op. cit.*, p. 209; in more dialectical terms, F. C. Baur, *op. cit.*, pp. 143f., 183, 309.

laid hold of in faith.[43] The community under the Word lives and
exists from the place granted to it in the presence of the Creator and
from its ever-new experience of the first day of creation in its own
life. This is the meaning of the dogmatic christology in our Gospel.
Therefore the perspective of saving history, not only of the cross,
Easter, Ascension and the Parousia, but also of the pre-Christian
epoch, is decisively foreshortened. Here lies the real difference
between him and Paul. For John, the presence of Christ extends
over all times because it is the presence of the Creator. Abraham
and Moses already saw his day, the day of his presence which began
with the creation. What formerly was veiled in heaven has now come
near and remains near in the voice of Jesus in the community. The
presence of Christ will find its conclusion, just as it has had a past.
But the eternal today, in which the light shines, can only with strain
and difficulty be arranged into epochs. The fact that God is present
and active, and appoints time, space and history, cannot, however,
itself be limited by temporal, spatial and historical categories. Consequently the proclamation is no longer in terms of history but in
terms of dogma. God's presence has burst open the realm of human
history and changes time and world into spheres in which the eternal
light shines into the earthly darkness.

John has developed and illustrated this viewpoint with examples.
The redactor who in 21.25 fell back upon and interpreted 20.30 has
understood him quite correctly. The occurrence which our Gospel
reports can never be narrated completely. John's Gospel is and
remains an abbreviation, and the same applies to his doctrine. His
doctrine provokes interpretation and kerygmatic unfolding instead
of freezing and absolutizing it. John employed many means to point
this out. He pictured Jesus in Hellenistic categories as miracle
worker, as saviour of the world and as pre-existent heavenly being.
But in the Hellenistic world there were many miracle-workers, sons
of God, and Jesus is something more than they. John also made use
of the Jewish categories of prophet, teacher and Messiah, but these
do not adequately disclose his cosmic significance. The symbols of
water, bread, light, truth, life, shepherd and door are best suited,
because every man has need of them and perishes without them. The
one who makes alive is at the same time the judge of the world which
rejects him. No one can reject him without choosing death by so
doing, and falling into delusion and darkness. Salvation and

---

[43] Compare Bultmann, *Evangelium*, p. 413, Brown, *op. cit.*, p. CXXI.

condemnation belong quite closely together here. The Johannine dualism receives its depth and cutting-edge from the fact that in the presence of the Creator, one can respond only with yes or no, and in so doing in the last analysis deny or affirm one's own existence.

When the community under the Word confesses the divinity of Jesus, then according to 17.3 it has eternal life, but only so long as it recognizes and declares anew what that means. It is never self-evident and never really preserved without being heard again and again and laid hold of repeatedly. We have to be reminded of this by means of polemic, since the world does not understand itself in the light of its Creator, but desires to live from itself, seeking its glory by itself. There are critical consequences even for the Church and in the Church. One can resist the presence of God in the Word by calling upon the fathers and upon former saving occurrences. One can set one's mind against the prophetic grasp of the Spirit by hiding in the fortifications of religiosity; this is what the Jews do, according to John. Then salvation history and the means of salvation become bulwarks of the pious man against the Creator, whom we need daily anew. Jesus is always an offence, too, and becomes a stumbling block even for his disciples. In distinction from Paul's view, the Johannine Christ becomes a stumbling-block, not on account of his cross and lowliness, but because, in the world which finds its self-understanding in itself, he proclaims the rightful sovereign claim of the Creator upon his creation and demands our obedience. As in Paul, so here man loses his own claim, his self-made rights and privileges, when the name of the Father is proclaimed, where man is placed into the state of the creature. The community under the Word is therefore always also the community in which the offence of the world is overcome. The eschatological creation can exist only in separation from the world.

IV

CHRISTIAN UNITY

THE UNITY OF Christianity has always been threatened. Occasionally the threat has been imposed from without, but it is always present from within. Christian unity exists concretely only so long as it remains a task to be fulfilled. Since uniformity cannot be a Christian solution, this task becomes all the more difficult. Neither the use of force nor the category of norm can fulfil the task, for the quest for unity can never consist in levelling off the differences. The multi-structured world can only be penetrated by the multi-structured gifts and ministries which proceed from the fullness of Christ's possibilities. Therefore, unity does not mean uniformity, but solidarity, the tension-filled interconnection between those who differ among themselves. Christian unity implies the freedom of the individual in the exercise of the gift and of the service entrusted to him. Thus it teaches men to tolerate and even to appreciate tensions, to avoid pressing everything into the same mould. This solidarity advocates freedom to the very limits of what would break up the fellowship. If it were otherwise, Christianity would become sterile and unfit for service. Therefore Christian unity must not merely be demanded, but also be rightly understood, rightly substantiated and taught. Every age in the history of the Church has endeavoured to do this. For this reason Paul described the Church as the Body of Christ. The admonition to preserve unity constituted the very core of the eucharistic exhortation which he adopted. Such admonitions gain importance through the growth of the Church in the succeeding generations. Now the horizon expands from the congregation in worship to world-wide Christendom whose coherence in time and space must be clarified. The Letter to the Ephesians has accomplished this in a daring design. John 17 is closely related to it. Here, too, the unity has been made into the dominant criterion of the true

Church and the key words through which the unity is described have become technical terms.

The background, as well as the impelling forces of this new phase of development in primitive Christian history, can be inferred from the carefully stylized tripartite acclamation in Eph. 4.5: 'One Lord, one faith, one baptism'. 'Faith' obviously refers here to the formulated confession. The administration of baptism in which this acclamation may originally have had its setting is now not merely the basis of the individual Christian's life, but rather, according to Eph. 5.26, the act out of which the Church itself grows. In the solemn confession, the Christian Church testifies to the basic factors of its origin and being. Because these basic factors are not subjected to earthly changes, they guarantee the unity of that community which exists under their control. An acclamation like this is meaningful only when imminent dangers are to be warded off through it. When the Church confesses that its unity is realized in heaven and perpetually guaranteed, it is obviously delimiting itself from heretics and their attempts induced by the 'Spirit' to dissolve it into sectarian fellowships. It is significant that we do not find here just an admonition to preserve the unity of the Christian brotherhood. Nor are the divisions and schisms any longer regarded from an apocalyptic viewpoint as signs of the great confusion of the end-times, as we find in I Cor. 11.19. Now factions are considered as a sacrilege against that fellowship which is grounded in heaven and which, according to I Tim. 3.15, is the pillar and bulwark of truth. That fellowship possesses unity essentially and intrinsically, namely as the mark of truth. In Eph. 4.5, a formative orthodoxy asserts itself which considers itself to be constitutively bound to heaven and in this respect to be the institution of salvation and not merely the instrument of grace. The unity of this orthodoxy now becomes identical with the truth of the right doctrine which it must administer as the mystery of divine revelation. Earthly reality may show its nature as dispersion and division. The heavenly reality is of necessity one and indivisible.

These preliminary remarks sketch the context in which John 17 must be seen. We can hardly understand this chapter and its concluding petition for unity unless we take into account the conflict within the Church which was almost universal at the end of the first century. The position of the Gospel is dominated by the fact that church unity here is not only based on heavenly realities but also deduced from the relationship of the Father to the Son and of the

Son to the Father and of both to the disciples. Of course, this can be understood as being a solemn comparison resulting from edifying rhetoric. However, if this is so, we fail to get a difficult theological problem into focus by hiding it behind clouds of pious verbiage. The emphasis then quite necessarily rests upon the demand for unity which the disciples themselves must realize. It is no longer clear that the summons to human effort is unimportant in the text. The Johannine Christ prays to God for unity rather than demanding it from men. Apparently the realization of unity does not lie in the hands of the disciples. If the prayer is also indirectly a summons, it reminds the disciples of their obligation to retain the gift which has been granted, for it can be lost through man's own fault. It is, however, of crucial importance to realize that unity can be testified to as the earthly mark of the Christian community only because unity is already prefigured in the relationship between the Father and the Son and because unity is transferred through the activity of the Father and the Son to the community. We would do well to ponder the strangeness of this mode of thinking. It is not sufficient to take only its theological scope seriously. We are here first of all confronted with a problem which needs to be discussed on the basis of the methodology of comparative religion. Without its solution, important connections and relations within this Gospel remain unclear.

If the disciples are drawn into the unity of the Father and the Son, then it is once again indicated that the ecclesiology is unfolded with the christology as its point of orientation and departure. This was already the case with the Pauline motif of the Church as the Body of Christ. John, however, goes further, in that he brings the Father directly into his ecclesiology and does not merely lay stress on the obedience of the servants and members of Christ. The mark of Christianity is its unity with its Lord and his Father. This implies that the motif of unity is not restricted to christology any more than christology is restricted to soteriology. If John is labelled a mystic as a result,[1] the real problem is being concealed behind a vague catchword. We must rather ask: In what sense can the key word unity embrace the Father, Son and the disciples in theological thought, and in which historical situation is this Johannine concept of unity possible? We must be careful that the differences between them are not blurred. Only arbitrariness could refuse to recognize the difference between the Father and the Son. Just as the Father remains superior

[1] Gaugler, *op. cit.*, p. 37.

to the Son even when the Son's divinity is stressed, so likewise both Father and Son remain superior to the community, even though the community reflects the divine relationship between the Father and the Son. Here, too, unity seems to mean the solidarity of differences. But in what sense is this so?

We usually bypass the question at this point with edifying language by reducing unity to what we call love.[2] The Gospel itself misleads us into doing just that because in 3.35; 10.17; 15.9; 17.23ff., John speaks of the Father's love for the Son; in 14.31 he refers to the Son's love for the Father, and correspondingly also speaks of the love of both for the community. Love and unity are here brought together and identified. Once again we have the appearance of a dialectical play with certain key words which aim to express the same subject-matter from different aspects. But this insight should protect us from indiscriminately connecting what must be kept distinct and oversimplifying the whole problem. What we quite vaguely call love must not rob the Johannine motif of its importance. If love should turn out to be the concrete expression of unity, unity still remains love's origin and basis. Distinctions like these indicate that the concept of love in the Fourth Gospel is not without problems. It is not even universally recognized that John demands love for one's brethren, but not for one's enemies, and correspondingly that Jesus loves his own, but not the world. This fact may not be diminished in importance by explaining it in the context of the situation of the farewell speeches, which are concerned with the existence of the circle of the disciples and with the preservation of Jesus' gift.[3] There is no indication in John that love for one's brother would also include love toward one's neighbour,[4] as demanded in the other books of the New Testament. On the contrary, John here sets forth an unmistakable restriction[5] such as we also know from the Qumran community,[6] and this also indicates the historical situation of our Gospel with unusual clarity.

It should not be overlooked that according to 3.16 God loved the world. But it is more than doubtful whether this statement, which is

---

[2] Compare H. Odeberg, *The Fourth Gospel* (1929), p. 114; Dodd, *Interpretation*, pp. 194–9; Barrett, *op. cit.*, p. 428; Michel, *op. cit.*, p. 532.

[3] Bultmann, *Evangelium*, p. 405; *Theologie*, p. 435 (ET II, p. 82).

[4] Contrary to Hoskyns, *op. cit.*, p. 451; Barrett, *op. cit.*, pp. 81f.

[5] So W. Bauer, *Johannesevangelium*, p. 248; Gaugler, *op. cit.*, pp. 218f.; Schweizer, *op. cit.*, p. 375 (ET, p. 238).

[6] Brown, *op. cit.*, p. LXIII.

nowhere repeated in John, should give us the right to interpret the whole Johannine proclamation from this perspective. According to the context, we have every reason to consider this verse as a traditional primitive Christian formula which the Evangelist employed.[7] Its sole purpose in John is to stress the glory of Jesus' mission, that is to say the miracle of the incarnation. References to God's love for the world are absent in Jesus' own witness to himself as well as in his commandment given to his disciples. It is just the same with the predication 'saviour of the world', which appears in 4.42 but does not adequately designate the Johannine Christ. To be sure, according to 3.17; 6.33; 12.47 Jesus is sent to save the world and to give it life and, according to 9.5; 12.46, he is the light of the world. But the Gospel shows that his mission results in the judgment of the world. It is not accidental, therefore, that the commandment of brotherly love is part of the esoteric instruction of the disciples and not without reason that we read in I John 2.15, in sharp contrast to John 3.16: 'If anyone loves the world, in him is not the love of the Father.' While the Johannine school is heard in I John 2.15, in this case it does not deviate from the teaching of John's Gospel which just as emphatically uses the hatred of the world as a contrasting background to the love within the community. This becomes even clearer when the concept of love in the Fourth Gospel is analysed without naïvely presupposing straight away that it means nothing more than normal ethical conduct.[8]

In 15.9ff., love is defined as the keeping of the commandments, and this definition of love applies to Jesus as well as to the disciples. According to 15.15, Jesus' love for his disciples is expressed by his communicating to them the word of the Father. Apparently the communication of the word to the disciples is also the essence of the Father's love for the community. Hence, we may infer that the Father's love for the Son from 'before the foundations of the world' which, according to 17.24, made him to be the Son and the revealer, can only mean that God has always spoken to Jesus. Therefore he is the exclusive and unique Word of God for the world. If this is so, then the conclusion seems inevitable: If Jesus sends his own into the world in order to speak the Word there and if in this proclamation the

[7] W. Bauer, *op. cit.*, p. 57; S. Schulz, *Untersuchungen zur Menschensohnschristologie im Johannesevangelium* (1957), p. 140; against this view, Bultmann, *Evangelium*, p. 110, n. 5.

[8] Contrary to Dodd, *Interpretation*, pp. 398f.; correctly, Bultmann, *Evangelium*, pp. 403f.

divine love is revealed, then the disciples' mission in the world, like Christ's own mission, bears the mark of divine love. It is surprising that this obvious and logical conclusion has nowhere explicitly been drawn. We have now reached one of the cruxes of Johannine inter- pretation. The understanding of the entire Gospel depends on how we now interpret this strange phenomenon and in what direction we move from there. To repeat our last result once more: Love in John is inseparably bound to the event of the Word, to speaking the Word on one hand and to receiving and preserving it on the other. This is just as true for the Father's relation to the Son as it is for the relation of both to the community. We should not be side-tracked from this insight by 10.17f., where the Father's love for the Son is based on the Son's free surrender of his life. John 15.13 takes up this idea again in the form of a proverb and thus emphasizes it. Undoubtedly John cannot conceive of love without selfless service and surrender,[9] and 13.1 shows that Jesus' service and surrender implies death. We may and should add that with this idea our Gospel follows primitive Christian traditions in which love consistently means existence for others. However, this is not the characteristic Johannine manner of speaking of love. As soon as John reflects on the nature of love, he shows that selfless service and surrender are connected with the Word. Even in 15.13, the connection is made between the Word, the commandment of Jesus and love as sacrifice. According to 10.18, Jesus follows the Father's commandment when he lays down his life of his own accord. The Father loves the Son by showing him all that he himself is doing (5.20).

For John, real communication is impossible without words, dis- cussion, dialogue and, conversely, he understands such dialogue as the communication of one's being and therefore as love. If we wanted to pursue this line of thought, we would have to discover that obedience for him is, at the very core, the 'yes' of our response to the Word that is heard, as is intimated already by the derivation of the Greek verb 'to obey' from the verb 'to hear'. At any rate, love in John means something other than an emotion and it transcends even the sphere of ethical decisions. Love does not merely respect the rights or the needs of the other person in personal conduct. Love speaks to the other person and thus communicates itself, or else it preserves what is heard and so accepts the self-disclosure of the other person also through its own deeds of love. Thus in the disciple, faith and love

[9] Faulhaber, *op. cit.*, pp. 37, 41; Haenchen, *op. cit.*, p. 212.

indeed coincide.[10] But it must be carefully considered whether this may be interpreted as constituting a material unity, so that the decision of faith for the Word that has been heard would be identical with the decision of love for the claim of one's brother. Such an interpretation could no longer be deduced from the divine relationship between Father and Son as demanded by the Johannine context. In it, love is not primarily concerned with the claim of the other person, but with the Word. Faith means the acceptance of the Word and love means self-surrender to the Word in service. This corresponds to the conduct of Jesus, who lets himself be guided by his Father's word, not, of course, as a believer, but as the revealer. He did not receive the Word of God in time, nor in conjunction with the alternative of unbelief. This even corresponds to the activity of God himself who, from the beginning, communicated himself in the Word. This Word is his self-disclosure and it is therefore taken up in the Gospel as the self-disclosure of Jesus. Because in Jesus the Word places us before God himself, it is called sanctifying truth. The Word gives eternal life because through Jesus it enables us to recognize the Father who alone can be eternal life. However, what places us before God also separates us from the world. It continues to separate us even when we are not taken out of the world. Thus the disciples are simultaneously the elect, the friends, the loved ones, as well as those who are the object of the world's hatred. The love of God cannot be connected with the love of the world. For love, in John, means the communion which is established through the Word and preserved by the Word. The world, however, does not exist in the communion of this Word, but, as the Gospel describes it, at best under its judgment, because it does not accept it. Consequently, it is not accidental that John never speaks of the new world, and not even of the new creation, even though the Church, which was in his time already engaged in world-wide mission work, could have been given this name. A characteristic trait of our Gospel is the tension between universalism and predestination.[11] Jesus is designated the 'saviour of the world', who has come not to judge but to save the world, yet it is only the believers, the elect, his own, who are in fact saved. May one really argue that the believers represent the world, because God's purpose and goal is directed to the world?[12] Some Johannine texts obviously point this way, as seems

---

[10] In opposition to Bultmann, *Evangelium*, p. 421.
[11] Barrett, *op. cit.*, p. 428.
[12] Faulhaber, *op. cit.*, p. 29; Bultmann, *Evangelium*, p. 382.

necessary whenever the idea of creation strongly influences the whole proclamation. On the other hand, the Johannine dualism is an insurmountable barrier for the idea that the disciples represent the world. The possibilities inherent in apocalypticism no longer have validity, even if traditional formulae and a few phrases here and there are distant reminders of it. John is a man between the times. He lives in the age of world-wide mission. Yet he is no longer interested in a new world and its proclamation, which may perhaps even appear to him as something fantastic and absurd. He recognizes the new creation only in the form of reborn disciples. They, however, no longer represent the earthly but the heavenly world and therefore they are not the representatives of a restored creation.

Nowhere in the New Testament do we meet a more rigorous dualism than in John. It is one of the odd and almost comical features of the history of Johannine interpretation that this writing should have been connected with the Ephesian presbyter who as a very old man could speak only about love. Not even Paul, with his outbursts of anger and his irony, exhibited the cutting iciness of the so-called apostle of love, shown already in his style. Of course the Johannine dualism has not been driven to its radical conclusions. For the Christian community unceasingly grows out of this world and the disciples are unceasingly being sent into the world. The world is the arena of divine history. It can be that arena because God has created it. On the other hand, one must be saved from the world and one is saved through hearing and receiving the Word. The Johannine dualism is certainly not a metaphysical dualism. Heaven and earth are not on principle and unalterably in opposition. The earth as the creation of God remains the realm of his call. But it would also be inexact to speak of a dualism of decision.[13] That faith and unbelief involve decision cannot be denied. However, it is not man's decision which brings about the great separation of the two realms. The Johannine dualism marks the effect of the Word in that world in which the light has always shone into the darkness. As specific decisions of individual men, faith and unbelief confirm the separation which already exists. The decisions for or against the Word constantly take place on an earth which has already been separated into two hostile spheres through the event of the Word. As in Paul, for instance in I Cor. 1.18ff.; II Cor. 2.15f., so also here the Word of God effects the final separation between life and death, truth and lie,

---

[13] Bultmann, *Theologie*, pp. 373, 429 (ET II, pp. 21, 76).

light and darkness, Church and world. As the Word of the Creator it unceasingly separates creation from chaos, as on the first day. Therefore, together with creation, the Word also brings about chaos. In this sense the Word effects all things. The Johannine dualism is nothing but the doctrine of the omnipotence of the Word. Nowhere else is the whole salvation and the whole condemnation more radically dependent on the hearing of the Word than in our Gospel. Just as the Word precedes faith, so also it continually brings out anew the quality of darkness, and of unbelief as remaining in darkness. Rebirth is quite impossible for human understanding, and even for Christian insight it remains a mysterious miracle, because the notion of a restored creation is given up. Faith arises only through the power and in the manner of the resurrection of the dead, but this is not effective everywhere. In Judaism as a whole, for instance, the resurrection power bounces off on the insurmountable rule of the power of death. There exists not merely the possibility that a man does not want to believe. There is also the other one, that he cannot believe. To decide in favour of Jesus is a divine gift and possible only for the elect. Conversely, in faith election becomes apparent and the divine gift is offered to everyone.

From this perspective John drew far-reaching consequences. The world-wide commission and mission of the Church and the duty of every individual believer to participate in it are all presupposed. The call to discipleship also includes being sent forth. Not even women are excluded. The obligation to do mission work knows no exceptions. In 17.18 the departing Christ summarizes this task once again as constituting his will, just as his own way on earth as the messenger of the Father stood under the same commandment and served as a heavenly example for his own. Christian life as such is mission. No one can say this more loudly and emphatically than John. This does not yet answer the question of the expectations and intentions that are connected with this task. It is of the utmost importance to recognize that here, too, the arena of the disciples' mission is not its goal, and the limitless scope of the task is not meant to produce or to give form to a new world. The disciples who are being sent into all the world are at the same time reminded that they themselves are not and cannot be of this world. So little are they a part of the world that in 17.15 the departing Christ must express his will, declaring that he does not want them to be taken out of this world. Their task leads them into the world which at its core is an alien realm for the disciples, just as, according to John, Jesus himself has been an alien sojourner in this world below. The paradox of the incarnation finds its extension in the Christian mission and receives its meaning anew there. Incarnation in John does not mean complete, total entry into the earth, into human existence, but rather the encounter between the heavenly and the earthly. For the disciples, as for Jesus, inasmuch as both are representatives of heaven, this world below is the realm of activity through which they must pass without establishing a permanent home in it. Actually the Christian mission according to John does not have validity for the world as such, but only for those who, being in the world, are given to Christ by his Father, in short to the elect who are called to faith. We do not know beforehand who belongs to this group or how many they are. This becomes evident in the reaction to the Word. Thus the world is the object of mission only in so far as it is necessary to gather the elect. John 11.52 expresses this idea unmistakably, transferring a part of the apocalyptic hope of Judaism into a new context. The scattered children of God must be gathered together. If this is the task of the disciples, then we understand why the object of Christian love in John is not one's neighbour as such. In practice, he may be that object, since the message is directed to all and since prior to the reaction of a man to the Word it is not decided whether or not he will be a brother. But what in a practical sense has always yet to be discovered, has, theologically and in principle, already been decided. The object of Christian love for John is only what belongs to the community under the Word, or what is elected to belong to it, that is, the brotherhood of Jesus.

Once again new light is shed on the historical situation of the Evangelist. One can hardly be unaware of a dogmatic hardening and contraction at this point. In the course of church history, it was usually the conventicles that considered the relationship between Church and world from this perspective. The earthly Jesus who went to publicans and sinners and who told the parable of the Good Samaritan is just as remote as the Pauline proclamation of the justification of the ungodly. This does not mean that John could not have pictured Jesus as a Good Samaritan, making him an example for us, nor does it mean that the Johannine community had no room for erstwhile sinners. The proclamation of rebirth outdoes the Pauline preaching of justification rather than falling behind it. The difference is not in regard to morality but instead in a different relation to the earthly reality. The message of the God who walks on the face of the earth finds its correspondence in the community which, being conscious of its mission, is without a feeling of solidarity for the world. The omnipotence of the Word is emphasized most strongly. However, this omnipotence which refers to the Creator's activity is not related to the world. Even when the omnipotence of the Word is regarded as having a world-wide scope, it is still limited to the experience of the individual and of the group. The notion of the liberated community takes the place of the concept of the new world. In John, overcoming no longer means the conquest and transformation of everyday earthly existence, but, in agreement with his christology, separation from an earth which as such no longer belongs to Christ. Individual people, who may be scattered across the face of the world, belong to him and in this sense they constitute a world-wide Church. When the title 'the spiritual Gospel' was attached to the Fourth Gospel it denoted a true insight, though one might argue about the propriety of the label. Even where the Logos, like Sophia, comes to his own and is rejected by his own, the idea does not produce the firm conviction of the Old Testament and the primitive Christian message that: 'The earth is the Lord's and the fullness thereof.' My key word, unreflected docetism, takes its point of orientation from here. John does not consider removing the marks and characteristics of creation from this earth. Nor, however, does he allow the earth really to remain creation nor does he orient it on its new creation, even though Old Testament and Jewish reminiscences still linger in his ear, and God's creative activity is of utmost importance to his theology. The problem of comparative religion which arises here cannot be pursued in this context. Thus we cannot decide how strong Qumran's influence is on John and whether John presupposes the beginnings of a Christian gnosticism or whether he contributes to its formation. The relationship to the world is, at any rate, quite similar in John and in gnosticism. Bousset's interpretation[14] may to a large extent be the product of his age, inadequate or even wrong. But Bousset did correctly point out the atmosphere of a Christian mystery-community which permeates John. Temporally and theologically John is separated from post-Easter apocalypticism and at most he took from it some themes which he then reinterpreted. Spatially, at least, he is remote from the beginnings of early Catholicism and theologically he does not share its trends

[14] *Kyrios Christos* (1921), pp. 154–83.

even though he shares a number of its premises. But he challenges all forms of Christianity which want to build their home on earth, and ironically it can be noted that it was precisely those forms of Christianity which did not comprehend his challenge or else sublimated it to the extreme. The question of the nature of John's 'spirituality' will largely remain an argument of terminology. Yet it can hardly be denied that at all times he gave strength and shelter to spiritualism within and without the Church.

Only now can it be stated what is meant by unity in our Gospel. Unity expresses the solidarity of the heavenly. But here above all we must delineate clearly, since the various emphases of the differing interpretations become quite apparent and at cross purposes with each other. In understandable reaction against earlier interpretations, modern Protestant studies on John, though by no means only Protestant studies, endeavour to ward off or at least to curb an approach to John in terms of metaphysical categories. The category of personality in manifold variations seems to offer itself as an appropriate key to John, though it would be rather difficult to define the nature of the heavenly personality when it is not easy to do so even with regard to the human personality. In theological language, so one might argue, the word love can never be wrong. John himself used it, indicating that love expresses and preserves the unity and conversely that unity is the presupposition as well as the result of love. Therefore interpreters declare that, 'the only kind of personal union . . . with which we are acquainted is love',[15] as if people could not also be united in dialogue or in common action. That love is God's own life and activity may, in view of the biblical proclamation of God as judge and Lord, hardly be regarded as being a general, more or less self-evident truth.[16] Finally, what does it mean to speak of our love for God or for Christ? To speak in terms of a 'real community of being, a sharing of life' with God,[17] remains quite obscure so long as the interpreter does not employ but, in liberalist fashion, dilutes the concept of *gratia infusa*, of infused grace. Others place in opposition or relate positively to each other 'metaphysical' and 'ethical' categories, so that, for instance, the ethical unity is substantiated by a metaphysical foundation.[18] When the trinitarian problem is not

---

[15] Dodd, *Interpretation*, p. 199.
[16] *Ibid.*, p. 196.
[17] *Ibid.*, p. 197.
[18] Hoskyns, *op. cit.*, pp. 389f.; W. Bauer, *Johannesevangelium*, p. 84.

ignored, the unity of will[19] is often made into the decisive feature and Jesus' obedience, to which our obedience must correspond, is then sharply accentuated.[20] If, on the other hand, the notion of the divine revealer is stressed,[21] there is a deliberate move away from an ethical interpretation in order to set forth the identity of Father and Son. In that case, of course, it is necessary to separate the statement of the unity of the community from the unity of the Father and the Son and to describe the former in terms of an inner unity in the tradition of the Word and of faith, or even as uniformity. But the unity of the community may not be detached from the unity of Father and Son which is its foundation. For John, unity is a mark and a quality of the heavenly realm in the same way in which truth, light and life are the quality and mark of the heavenly reality. Therefore unity cannot be interpreted on the basis of earthly analogies like friendship or covenant, nor may it be reduced to a uniformity of will. Unity in our Gospel exists only as heavenly reality and therefore in antithesis to the earthly, which bears the mark of isolations, differences and antagonisms.[22] If unity exists on earth, then it can only exist as a projection from heaven, that is, as the mark and object of revelation.

John is not content with simply stating unity as a fact. He also sees it rooted in certain relations and the interpretation of those relations is the real problem of our texts. It is typical for these relations that a heavenly gradation, a process through a series of stages, unites the superior with the inferior. We also meet this notion in Ephesians. Thus the controversial passage Eph. 3.15 carries force only if all earthly fatherhood has its prototype in the divine fatherhood and is derived from it. Still more clearly, in Eph. 5.25ff., the relationship between Christ and the Church serves as the model for Christian marriage. This marriage represents the mystery of the perfect union announced in Gen. 2.24. The word 'model' is, of course, too modern, since more than merely an example or a norm is implied here. We are rather dealing with the reflection of the heavenly reality in the earthly counterpart and the participation, arranged in gradations, of the earthly counterpart in the nature of the heavenly prototype. Thus the sequence, given by Paul in I Cor. 11.3ff., of God, Christ, man, woman does not refer by accident to gradations of heavenly glory.

[19] C. Maurer, *Ignatius von Antiochien und das Johannesevangelium* (1949), p. 60f.; Michel, *op. cit.*, p. 532; Barrett, *op. cit.*, p. 428.

[20] Hirsch, *op. cit.*, pp. 377ff.; Haenchen, *op. cit.*, pp. 215f.

[21] Bultmann, *Evangelium*, pp. 187f.; 392f.

[22] Compare the excellent interpretation in Odeberg, *op. cit.*, pp. 113f.

Heaven here is not a realm closed in itself, for the heavenly reality invades the earth with explosive power in order to unfold itself in representations as its earthly counterparts. While those representations no longer possess the full reality of their heavenly origin, they still participate in it in degree. The successions of emanations in later gnosticism are based on the same notions. Yet nowhere else in the New Testament do such ideas have greater significance than in John. His symbolic discourses are determined by them, for they are based on the premise that the earthly things, such as earthly bread, light, etc., have their truth in the heavenly prototype. Therefore, what is earthly becomes a phantom of salvation if it becomes the object of human longing. The earthly counterpart may not be isolated from the full reality of its origin. While it has no lifegiving powers in itself, its significance lies in the fact that it can be a sign pointing to the heavenly reality.

This is the context in which John's view of Christian unity belongs. Unity on earth exists only as a reflection and an extension of heavenly reality. Therefore it can exist only within that realm which can reflect the heavenly reality, namely the realm of the divine Word. The relationship of the Father to the Son and of the Son to the Father is the prototype of true solidarity. There the Word is spoken and received, that Word which is the beginning and the end of salvation, since God reveals himself in it. Out of this solidarity the Word is revealed through Christ to the world so that God himself becomes manifest as Creator. The community under the Word is his creation and remains his creation so long as it remains under the Word that is continually addressed to it anew. The community, like the first creation, cannot live from itself. But in so far as it lives from the Word, it lives from heaven even while on earth, being drawn into the community between Father and Son. Because of this, the community itself is a heavenly reality. This idea is expressed in the most astonishing form in 10.34f. There the statement of Ps. 82.6, 'You are gods', is justified through the reception of the divine Word. To be sure, the verse has a christological slant, but it cannot be limited to christology only, since it already had validity for the community of the old covenant. The accepted Word of God produces an extension of heavenly reality on earth, for the Word participates in the communion of Father and Son. This unity between Father and Son is the quality and mark of the heavenly world. It projects itself to the earth in the Word in order to create the community there which, through rebirth from above, becomes integrated into the unity of Father and Son. This almost frightening understanding of the Johannine community must be called gnosticizing. Here one perceives most clearly John's naïve docetism which extends to his ecclesiology also. His interpretation of the Old Testament is also gnosticizing, and this does not merely apply to the above-quoted text.[23] This kind of approach to the Old Testament has nothing to do with the historical Jesus. In these verses there speaks the one whom John 1.18 calls the exegete of the invisible God, on whose bosom and in unity with whom he remains even while on earth. He is the Logos to whom, according to 1.51, even in his earthly existence the angels of God descend and from whom they ascend, thus demonstrating for the eyes of the believers his unbroken contact with the heavenly world. In his function as the revealer, Jesus is all that the 'I am' words declare him to be. Therefore the earthly community participates in the heavenly world through him as he speaks to it. This is not only true for the whole of Christianity; it is no less true for the individual members and their reciprocal relationship. Brotherly love is all that is needed, for brotherly love means seeing one's brother as existing under the Word of God, receiving him through the Word and giving him the possibility of remaining under the Word. Brotherly love is heavenly solidarity directed towards individual Christians. Finally, Christian mission is solidarity in the process of seeking out brothers through the proclamation of the Word which proceeded from God to Christ and thence to the community. The purpose of missionary proclamation is to gain the outsider as a brother. The assertion of 4.35, that the fields are already ripe for the harvest, applies to this seeking out in missionary work.

John's idea of mission is the reinterpretation of an apocalyptic motif. This insight can serve as a transition for our next affirmation, that the catchword 'realized eschatology' does not fully do justice to John, in spite of the fact that John placed the *praesentia Christi* in the centre of his proclamation. On the basis of his presuppositions, John developed something like a unique futurist eschatology and John 17 indicates that the Evangelist not only focussed his attention upon the past and the present but that he also possessed a future hope. It is no longer the hope held in the period immediately following Easter. John, along with early Catholicism, shares the perspective held by a time which is no longer overshadowed by the imminent *eschaton*.

[23] Compare Dahl, *op. cit.*, pp. 141f.

For him, as well as for early Catholicism, the decisive event had already taken place and was now being developed within Christianity's sphere of influence. For John it was not being developed in the form of a church organization, but rather as the encounter with Jesus and his Word. This difference does not change the Evangelist's understanding of the time and situation in which he found himself. On the other hand, it would be false to argue that his understanding reckoned simply with an endless stretch of time and its inevitable developments. Not even the early Catholic Church held this view, for it never surrendered the idea of the end, however often the idea grew pale and became insignificant. John 17.20ff. shows that John, on the basis of his own theological premises, did hold a futurist eschatological expectation. It represents a modification of the Church's tradition, but his expectation for the future is urgent nevertheless.

The petition for unity is now varied because attention is focussed on those who come to faith in the future through the Christian proclamation of the Word. The formula which in 4.39 referred to the proclamation to the Samaritans is now applied to them. The first generation is united with those still to come under the Word, and each generation has its peculiar advantage and bears its special risk. While the first disciples had the advantage of coming to Jesus in person, they did not know and could not yet see the world-wide witness of the succeeding community in which the glory of Jesus extends itself. And while that world-wide witness opens the door to Jesus more easily for later generations, they in turn are in greater danger of being subjected to a proclamation which, according to 4.43, can become sheer idle talk. Thus Jesus' petition must enclose all, and he prays here for all with the oft-quoted words 'that they may all be one'. This is not edifying rhetoric, as most interpreters suppose. If my previous analysis was correct, then John here speaks of the gathering under the dominion of the Word of what belongs to heaven. The same idea is stated in 10.16 with the formula of the 'one flock and one shepherd'. John 17.23 repeats, slightly modifying the expression, 'that they may be perfected into unity'. Perfection in John means that the perils are past and overcome. The gathering of the community points to a goal, and that goal is free from earthly perils. Once more this idea is restated by the following verse (17.24): It is the will of Jesus that all who are his should be with him in that heavenly place where he is and there behold his eternal glory. This heavenly place is, according to 14.2f., his Father's house with many rooms, which Jesus no longer needs to prepare for his own because the Father has done so already. John 12.32 promised the disciples that the exalted Lord would draw them to himself into his heavenly glory.

We have seen that only a few texts contain the futurist eschatology which is peculiar to John. But these texts gain unusual importance as soon as we compare them with the futurist eschatology of the Synoptics or of Paul. The fact that this futurist hope is simply taken for granted in John, that it is expressed almost incidentally and emphasized only at the end of chapter 17 makes his hope all the more significant. For the disciples of Jesus on earth the goal of the sojourn is the final unification of the community in heaven, where, like its Lord, the community too is removed from earthly persecution.[24] Of course, John 14.2f. does not mean that in the hour of death, Jesus brings his own to himself,[25] or else 17.24 would also have to be understood in this fashion.[26] Nor, however, does the Johannine Jesus refer to a cosmic process in which humanity is called and gathered to unity with God.[27] Rather, John spiritualized old apocalyptic traditions. The point of departure for primitive Christian apocalypticism and especially of the post-Easter ecclesiology was the hope of the gathering of the scattered tribes of Israel or of the rebuilding of Israel on the basis of a remnant. For the present we cannot show how primitive Christian apocalypticism developed into the Johannine reinterpretation. But we can note that the Jewish-Christian hope has been transposed from the earthly realm into the metaphysical dimension.[28] In place of the scattered people of God we find the children of God scattered throughout the world; in place of the earthly kingdom with its eschatological Zion we find unification in heaven. As in II Peter 1.11, the ingathering of the faithful into the eternal kingdom takes the place of Christ's *parousia* for the final judgment. In all such modifications the notion of the gathering of the elect is present. This notion is united in John with the idea found, for

---

[24] W. Bauer, *Johannesevangelium*, pp. 178f.; Barrett, *op. cit.*, p. 429.
[25] Bultmann, *Evangelium*, p. 465, n. 1.
[26] So Bultmann, *Evangelium*, p. 399.
[27] Faulhaber, *op. cit.*, p. 58; Michel, *op. cit.*, p. 533; Thüsing's interpretation, pp. 23f., of the gathering around the cross is absurd.
[28] This is different in Bultmann, *Theologie*, p. 444 (ET II, p. 92), who speaks of the reality of the Invisible Church in the Visible Church. Gaugler, *op. cit.*, pp. 209f., 216, presents a similar view, though from different presuppositions.

instance, in Ephesians, that in the Church the heavenly unification is already taking place and is growing in a world-wide dimension. Thus the perfection of the unification is but the end and goal of the eschatological process which is already in motion. What is heavenly cannot remain on earth, even though it must be gathered on earth. If we formulate our result in this way, then it becomes apparent that John prepares for the gnostic proclamation or else already stands under its influence. For gnosticism regards the gathering of the souls scattered on earth as the goal of world history. The gnostic problem does not appear just with the original circulation and use of the Fourth Gospel. It is already raised by the whole of Johannine eschatology. The outstanding marks of Johannine eschatology are (1) its transformation into protology; (2) the consistent presentation of Jesus as God walking on the face of the earth; (3) the ecclesiology of the community which consists of individuals who are reborn through the divine call, which lives from the Word, and which represents the heavenly unification on earth; (4) the understanding of the world and of the community's mission; (5) the reduction of Christian exhortation to brotherly love, and (6), finally, the hope of heavenly perfection. These characteristic marks of Johannine eschatology dovetail perfectly with each other and should not be interpreted in isolation from each other. The Johannine problem may not be cut up into a series of minor problems, but must be seen as a whole. Of course, each detail is important, but the whole may not be dissolved into details to the extent that one cannot see the wood for the trees. The Johannine problem as a whole, however, exhibits more than a temporal distance from the post-Easter Church and thus a closeness to the rising early Catholicism.[29] It also exhibits a contrast with early Catholicism shown by a conventicle with gnosticizing tendencies.

[29] Gaugler, *op. cit.*, p. 42, saw this most clearly when he spoke of a forerunner of a naturally 'pure' Catholicism.

V

CONCLUSION

THE RESULT FORMULATED in the previous paragraph differs greatly from traditional church views, as well as from the interpretation of John prevalent today. If one is aware of the almost desperate endeavours during the past century of investigations into the most difficult of all New Testament problems, which have resulted in a constant succession of new approaches and the postulation of endless new theses, one will also retain a critical stance towards one's own proposed solution. We can only say which questions and which possibilities we have recognized. Whether with our viewpoints and the results thus gained we will succeed in finding common approval is not decisive for scholarship. What is important is only that new questions again force us to engage in further reflection and teach us to listen to the texts anew. In order for this to be done rightly, we must be clear about the implication of an interpretation which departs from the customary approach. Some concluding remarks are meant to give some guidance for this.

Hardly any other writing in the New Testament has exercised as much fascination as John both inside and outside the Church throughout the centuries. Those who found Christ's true voice in it and called it, in distinction from the Synoptics, the spiritual Gospel, acknowledged the claim raised by the Gospel itself. Yet its inclusion in the canon is not without irony. The Gospel of John was called the heavenly Gospel because the Church which included it in the canon no longer knew John's earthly, historical situation, and it employed legends of apostolic authorship here as elsewhere in order to cover up its ignorance. Neither apostolic authorship nor apostolic content can be affirmed for it, despite the efforts of apologetics to this very day. The criterion of apostolicity contradicts the Johannine insight that earthly tradition as such is always incapable of legitimating the Christian witness. For John, all earthly tradition has a right to exist only if it serves the voice of Jesus, and it must be examined accordingly. If historically the Gospel reflects that development which led from the enthusiasts of Corinth and of II Tim. 2.18 to Christian gnosticism, then its acceptance into the Church's canon took place through man's error and God's providence. Against all its own intentions, and misled by the picture of Jesus as God walking on the face of the earth, the Church assigned to the apostles the voice of those whom it otherwise ignored and one generation later condemned as heretics.[1] The label 'heavenly' was attached to the Gospel which

---

[1] The above formulation is intentionally open to that kind of criticism which was made on the occasion of the republication of Walter Bauer's book, *Rechtgläubigkeit und Ketzerei im ältesten Christentum*. H. D. Altendorf's criticisms of Bauer and his successors, including myself, in his review in *ThLZ* (see Bibliography) are fundamental, striking and typical. I agree that it is indeed lamentable if by our doing 'the primitive Christian history threatens to dissolve into some sort of wild mish-mash of conflicting and mutually exclusive theological trends'. The criticism by the church historian of my at times disagreeable and always contestable results is well known to me, and I am even more aware of the uneasiness about my exegetical methodology. But are Altendorf and almost all the other opponents of Bauer's basic approach aware of the difficult situation in which the New Testament exegete, in distinction from other exegetes and historians, finds himself? Our work is carried out within a field of 657 pages of Nestle text which represents the fragment of a history of almost one hundred years. Eighteen hundred years of exegesis have investigated each line and each syllable from all possible perspectives, reading it backwards and forwards, turning it upside down, comparing it and raising one question after another. It is easy for outsiders to ridicule us, that we think we can hear the grass grow and the bedbugs cough. But what else should we try to do in the light of the situation with which we are confronted? It is easy to declare that 'a truly historical understanding cannot be gained in this manner'. If only it were clear what is meant by a 'truly historical understanding'! The historian who has a bird's-eye view of two thousand years of history will, even if he analyses individual texts, be able to see other perspectives, in contrast to the historian who crawls on his belly from molehill to molehill investigating the tiniest detail. The former sees as continuous what for the latter dissolves into a 'wild mish-mash'. Furthermore, the historian with the bird's-eye view is also confronted not only by the spirit in history, but also by every-day existence, which is usually more or less confusing and contradictory. Finally, for us who have learned from Bauer and Bultmann to be told by someone within the academic community that earlier exegetes of the New Testament had a closer relationship to the Church than we seem to have is a bit much! We spent half a lifetime in the pastorate and were formed by it. Again, we may be permitted to ask, which Church is actually meant? We ourselves have experienced to our sorrow 'the wild mish-mash' in the Church and we are therefore aware of ecclesiastical mythology and the legends which continue to grow exuberantly even since 1945. On the basis of our experiences within the Church, we as exegetes tend toward criticism of the tradition. Can we not postulate at least as a possible working hypothesis that the every-day life of primitive Christianity was determined by similar realities which also produced a 'wild mish-mash'? We do not operate completely without practical experience, even if some no longer remember and others do not want to know.

could no longer be located in time and space. The Church could no longer localize what had originated apart from or had run against the current of the broad stream which led to early Catholicism. However, the reception of the Fourth Gospel into the canon is but the most lucid and most significant example of the integration of originally opposing ideas and traditions into the ecclesiastical tradition. Pauline terminology and impulses had already taken up catchwords of his opponents. Later Hellenistic enthusiasts furnished material and points of argumentation for the opposing party, as can be concluded from the deutero-Pauline epistles and especially from the Letter of Jude. Early Catholicism as well as the canon did not originate without the influence of those trends which, since the end of the first century, were already considered by many as being heretical and thus were rejected.

With this we encounter the theological problem of the canon of the New Testament. It exists only as a diverse entity with many theological contradictions in which the complicated history of primitive Christianity is reflected. By affirming the canon we also acknowledge its divergent trends and even its contradictions. This cannot, however, imply that everything in it must be regarded as having equal validity or else be harmonized into a normative theology in which the divergencies are levelled off. While we have little right to reduce the canon within the Old or New Testament, because of its inner differences and divergences we are continually compelled to engage in new interpretations, decisions born out of our own hearing of the texts. The authority of the canon is never greater than the authority of the Gospel which should be heard from it.

Which authority, then, does belong to the Gospel of John? The inclusion of this book in the canon does not answer this question once and for all, especially since the Fourth Gospel itself has no conception of closed revelation, but rather advocates, even against itself, the ongoing operation of the Spirit's witness.[2] From the historical viewpoint, the Church committed an error when it declared the Gospel to be orthodox. Was this, from a theological viewpoint, a fortunate error? We cannot give an answer without first knowing what 'Gospel' means. But, on the other hand, the hermeneutical circle does not tell us about that. We rather have to hear the Gospel afresh, again by listening to John. Of course, this does not mean that leaping from one position to another, we could always postpone a decision about

[2] Gaugler, op. cit., p. 193.

the meaning of the Gospel and therefore avoid all dogmatic statements. There is not only the threat of dogmatic security, but also
the opposite threat, of a theological existence which is delivered
up to the impulses and whims of the moment, no longer knowing
anything except what can just as well be found outside the canon.
That someone preaches is meaningful only when he knows to some
extent *what* he must preach and what he may not preach. The fear
of dogmatism misled modern Protestantism into the tyranny of
arbitrary interpretations, and this threat is still greater today, in
spite of all attempts at theological repristination, than the threat
from the dogma which is not merely the result of blind assent and the
sacrifice of the intellect. Many sacrifices are offered to folly today on
many altars by those who are in agreement on only one point,
namely, that one altar, the altar of dogma, must be abolished at all
costs. Certainly faith and interpretation never exist otherwise than
in human entanglement and disorder. This is just as true for those
who receive the truth from a fixed dogmatic system as for those who
are misled into becoming theological vagabonds through the adven-
ture of exegesis. In the first case as well as in the second superstition
is celebrating its triumphs. Much would have been won if we became
aware of the dilemma and saw ourselves set in a twofold struggle. At
least the struggle against two opponents is typical for the majority of
New Testament writings, including our Gospel. John looks both
backwards and forwards,[3] and he proclaims his message as much in
dogmatic polemical form as in prophetic adaption of originally
enthusiastic traditions. As an historical phenomenon, the Fourth
Gospel also stands in the twilight and is subjected to human entanglement from which theological existence cannot remove itself. Is the
naïve docetism into which it slipped more harmless than the sacramental institution from which it disengaged itself? Did our Gospel
at least know the way of answering questions such as these, when it
demanded that we must continually surrender ourselves anew to the
Word of Jesus, when it evaluated every church in the light of the one
question, do we know Jesus?

Here our final problem arises. John 17 certainly does not contain
the words of the earthly Jesus, who was so thoroughly undocetic. The
question arises: What is the relationship between the exalted Christ
who is proclaimed here and the earthly Jesus? Can the Johannine
claim be defended that here the last, the ultimate testament of Jesus is

[3] Gaugler, *op. cit.*, p. 41.

being heard? The answer to this question depends on who Jesus is for us and whether he and he alone does lead us to the Father. It is precisely John's fascinating and dangerous theology that calls us into our creatureliness through his christological proclamation. In doing so, does he not also actually show us the one final testament of the earthly Jesus and his glory?

BIBLIOGRAPHY

T. ARVEDSON, *Das Mysterium Christ: Eine Studie zu Mt. 11.25–30* (Acta Seminarii Neotestamentici Upsaliensis 7), 1937.

H. D. ALTENDORF, Review in *ThLZ* 91 (1966), cols. 192ff., of Walter Bauer, *Rechtgläubigkeit und Ketzerei im ältesten Christentum,* q.v.

C. K. BARRETT, *The Gospel according to St John: An Introduction with Commentary and Notes on the Greek Text* (London: 1955).

W. BAUER, *Das Johannesevangelium* (HzNT 6), 3rd ed., 1933.
Rechtgläubigkeit und Ketzerei im ältesten Christentum, 2nd ed. with supplement by G. Strecker (Tübingen: 1964); ET, ed. R. Kraft and G. Krodel (Philadelphia: 1969).

F. C. BAUR, *Kritische Untersuchungen über die kanonischen Evangelien, ihr Verhältnis zueinander, ihren Charakter und Ursprung* (Tübingen: 1847).

W. BOUSSET, *Kyrios Christos: Geschichte des Christusglaubens von den Anfängen des Christentums bis Irenaeus* (FRLANT, NF 4, 2nd ed., 1921).

R. E. BROWN, *The Gospel according to St John,* Vol. I (chs. 1–12): Introduction, Translation and Notes (The Anchor Bible 29, New York: 1966).

R. BULTMANN, *Das Evangelium des Johannes* (KeK 2, 10th ed., 1941) (cited as *Evangelium*).
Theologie des Neuen Testaments, 5th ed. (Tübingen: 1965) (cited as *Theologie*); ET of 1st ed. by K. Grobel: *Theology of the New Testament* (New York and London: Vol. I, 1951; Vol. II, 1955).

O. CULLMANN, *Urchristentum und Gottesdienst,* 2nd ed. (Zürich: 1950); ET by A. S. Todd and J. B. Torrance: *Early Christian Worship* (SBT 10, 1953).

N. A. DAHL, 'The Johannine Church and History', *Current Issues in New Testament Interpretation: Essays in Honor of Otto Piper,* ed. W. Klassen and G. F. Snyder (New York and London: 1962), pp. 124–42.

C. H. DODD, *The Interpretation of the Fourth Gospel* (Cambridge: 1955) (cited as *Interpretation*).
Historical Tradition in the Fourth Gospel (Cambridge: 1963) (cited as *Tradition*).

J. DUPONT, *Essais sur la Christologie de Saint Jean* (Bruges: 1951).

D. FAULHABER, *Das Johannesevangelium und die Kirche* (Dissertation, University of Heidelberg: 1935; also Kassel: 1938).

E. GAUGLER, 'Die Bedeutung der Kirche in den johanneischen Schriften', *Internationale kirchliche Zeitschrift* 14 (Bern: 1924), pp. 97–117 and 181–219; *ibid.,* 15 (1925), pp. 27–42.

J. GRILL, *Untersuchungen über die Entstehung des 4. Evangeliums* (Vol. I, Tübingen and Leipzig: 1902; Vol. II, Tübingen: 1923).

E. HAENCHEN, 'Der Vater, der mich gesandt hat', *NTS* 9 (1962–3), pp. 208–16.

H. HEGERMANN, *Die Vorstellung vom Schöpfungsmittler im hellenistischen Judentum und Urchristentum* (TU 82, 1961).

W. HEITMÜLLER, *Das Johannesevangelium* (Die Schriften des Neuen Testaments 4, ed. J. Weiss), 3rd. ed. (Göttingen: 1918).

E. HIRSCH, *Das vierte Evangelium in seiner ursprünglichen Gestalt verdeutscht und erklärt* (Tübingen: 1936).

E. C. HOSKYNS, *The Fourth Gospel*, ed. F. N. Davey, 2nd ed. (London: 1947).

J. JEREMIAS, *Die Abendsmahlworte Jesu*, 3rd ed. (Göttingen: 1960); ET with the author's revisions to 1964 by N. Perrin: *The Eucharistic Words of Jesus* (London and New York: 1966).

E. KÄSEMANN, 'Aufbau und Anliegen des johanneischen Prologs', *Libertas Christiana: Festschrift für F. Delekat* (Munich: 1957), pp. 75–99; reprinted in *Exegetische Versuche und Besinnungen*, Vol. II (Göttingen: 1964), pp. 155–80. References are to the latter.

H. KÖSTER, 'Geschichte und Kultus im Johannesevangelium und bei Ignatius von Antiochen', *ZThK* 54 (1957), pp. 56–69; ET by A. Bellinzoni: 'History and Cult in the Gospel of John and in Ignatius of Antioch', *JThC* 1 (vol. entitled *The Bultmann School of Biblical Interpretation: New Directions*), ed. R. W. Funk (1965), pp. 111–23.

A. KRAGERUD, *Der Lieblingsjünger im Johannesevangelium: Ein exegetischer Versuch* (Oslo and Hamburg: 1959).

E. LOHSE, 'Wort und Sakrament im Johannesevangelium', *NTS* 7 (1960–1), pp. 110–25.

A. LOISY, *Le quatrième Évangile*, 2nd ed. (Paris: 1921).

T. W. MANSON, *On Paul and John* (SBT 38, 1963).

C. MAURER, *Ignatius und das Johannesevangelium* (Abhandlungen zur Theologie Alten und Neuen Testaments 18, Zürich: 1949).

O. MICHEL, 'Das Gebet des scheidenden Erlösers', *ZsystTh* 18 (1941), pp. 521–34.

F. MUSSNER, 'Die johanneischen Parakletsprüche und die apostolische Tradition', *BZ*, NF 5 (1961), pp. 56–70.

H. ODEBERG, *The Fourth Gospel: Interpreted in its Relation to the Contemporaneous Religious Currents in Palestine and the Hellenistic-Oriental World* (Uppsala: 1929).

F. OVERBECK, *Das Johannesevangelium: Studien zur Kritik seiner Erforschung*, ed. A. Bernoulli (Tübingen: 1911).

A. SCHLATTER, *Der Evangelist Johannes: Wie er spricht, denkt und glaubt. Ein Kommentar zum vierten Evangelium*, 2nd ed. (Stuttgart: 1948).

R. SCHNACKENBURG, *Das Johannesevangelium: I. Teil: Einleitung und Kommentar zu Kap. 1–4* (Herders theologischer Kommentar zum Neuen Testament 4, Freiburg and New York: 1965).
Die Kirche im Neuen Testament: Ihre Wirklichkeit und theologische Deutung, ihr Wesen und Geheimnis (Quaestiones Disputatae 14, Freiburg and New York: 1961); ET by W. J. O'Hara: *The Church in the New Testament* (New York: 1965).
'Der Menschensohn im Johannesevangelium', *NTS* 11 (1964–5), pp. 123–37.

S. SCHULZ, *Untersuchungen zur Menschensohn-Christologie im Johannesevangelium: Zugleich ein Beitrag zur Methodengeschichte der Auslegung des 4.
Evangeliums* (Göttingen: 1957).

E. SCHWEIZER, 'Der Kirchenbegriff im Evangelium und den Briefen des
Johannes', *Studia Evangelica: Papers Presented to the International Congress
on 'The Four Gospels in 1957' held at Christ Church, Oxford, in 1957* (TU 73,
1959), pp. 363–81; also in: E. Schweizer, *Neotestamentica* (Zürich and
Stuttgart: 1963), pp. 254–71; ET in *New Testament Essays: Studies in
Memory of T. W. Manson*, ed. A. J. B. Higgins (Manchester: 1959), pp.
230–45.

E. STAUFFER, *Die Theologie des Neuen Testaments*, 4th ed. (Stuttgart: 1948);
ET by J. Marsh: *New Testament Theology* (London and New York:
1955).

H. STRATHMANN, *Das Evangelium nach Johannes* (NTD 4), 7th ed.; 2nd ed.
of the new revision (1954).

W. THÜSING, *Die Erhöhung und Verherrlichung Jesu im Johannesevangelium*
(Neutestamentliche Abhandlungen 21, Münster, 1960).

R. WALKER, 'Jüngerwort und Herrenwort', *ZNW* 57 (1966), pp. 49–54.

J. WELLHAUSEN, *Das Evangelium Johannis* (Berlin: 1908).

G. P. WETTER, *Der Sohn Gottes: Eine Untersuchung über den Charakter und die
Tendenz des Johannesevangeliums* (FRLANT, NF 9, 1916).

W. WILCKENS, *Die Entstehungsgeschichte des vierten Evangeliums* (Zürich:
1958).

INDEX OF SUBJECTS

INDEX OF MODERN AUTHORS

INDEX OF BIBLICAL REFERENCES